Essential Histories: War and Conflict in Modern Times

The Iran–Iraq War

New York

Efraim Karsh

This edition published in 2009 by:

The Rosen Publishing Group, Inc.
29 East 21st Street
New York, NY 10010

First published in paperback in 2002 as Essential Histories 20 The Iran-Iraq War 1980–1988, © 2002 Osprey Publishing Limited.
Additional end matter copyright © 2009 by The Rosen Publishing Group, Inc.

Editor: Rebecca Cullen
Design: Ken Vail Graphic Design
Cartography by: The Map Studio
Index by: Susan Williams

Picture research by: Image Select International (p. 28 © Francoise De Mulder/Roger Viollet/Getty Images; p. 56 © Marco Di Lauro/ Getty Images)

Origination by PPS Grasmere, Ltd.

Library of Congress Cataloging-in-Publication Data

Karsh, Efraim.
The Iran-Iraq war / Efraim Karsh.
     p. cm.—(Essential histories)
Includes bibliographical references and index.
ISBN-13: 978-1-4358-7499-2 (library binding: alk. paper)
1. Iran-Iraq War, 1980–1988. I. Title.
DS318.85.K37 2008
955.05'42--dc22

                                                                                                    2008014885

Manufactured in the United States of America

Contents

The Middle East 1980

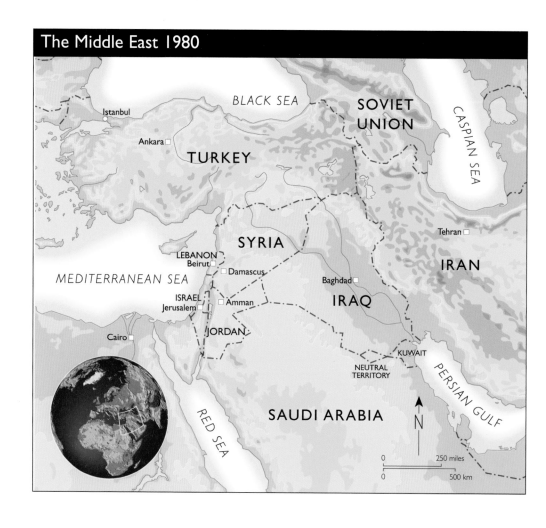

BLACK SEA

SOVIET UNION

CASPIAN SEA

Istanbul

Ankara

TURKEY

SYRIA

Tehran

LEBANON
Beirut

Damascus

Baghdad

IRAN

MEDITERRANEAN SEA

ISRAEL
Jerusalem

Amman

IRAQ

Cairo

JORDAN

KUWAIT

NEUTRAL
TERRITORY

PERSIAN GULF

RED SEA

SAUDI ARABIA

N

0   250 miles
0   500 km

Introduction

In most discussions of the Iran–Iraq War, it has become commonplace to view the conflict as the latest manifestation of the millenarian Arab–Persian struggle for domination of the Gulf and the Fertile Crescent. Some historians have traced its origins to the pre-Islamic rivalry between the Achaemenid and the Babylonian empires, others to the 7th-century Arab–Muslim destruction of the Sassanid Empire and the subsequent conversion of most Persians to Islam. Still others view the war as the extension of the historic struggle for power and control between Sunni and Shi'ite Islam: while Arabs are predominantly Sunni, with their emphasis on the Koran and the religious law, Iranians were converted in the 16th century to Shi'ism, a minority faction in Islam dating back to Ali Ibn-Abi-Talib, Prophet Muhammad's cousin and son-in-law.

Yet while these general causes may explain why wars between Iran and Iraq are possible, or even probable, they do not explain the occurrence of a specific war, let alone the lengthy periods of tranquility between the two countries. To understand why the Iran-Iraq War broke out in September 1980, it is necessary to look for more proximate causes, namely the nature of the two leaderships at the time and their political and ideological objectives.

Iran and Iraq: the historical legacy

This is all the more important given the fact that the periods of convergence and co-operation between 20th-century Iran and Iraq far exceeded those of hostilities and antagonism. During the late 1920s and the early 1930s, Iraq and Iran collaborated in quelling ethnic insurgencies in both countries. In 1937 they resolved their dispute over the strategic Shatt al-Arab waterway, separating Iraq from Iran at the head of the Gulf, and the same year established a regional security defense alliance ("the Saadabad Pact"), together with Turkey and Afghanistan. In 1955 the two, together with Britain, Turkey and Pakistan, established the Western-orchestrated Baghdad Pact for regional defense, and, with the exception of *ad hoc* brief crises, maintained working relations well into the late 1960s.

This peaceful co-existence was temporarily upset in the early 1970s. Because of a series of events—the announcement in 1968 of Britain's intention to withdraw from its military bases east of Suez, the diminution of a direct Soviet threat following the significant improvement in Iranian–Soviet relations beginning in the early 1960s, and rising oil revenues—the Iranian Shah, Mohammed Reza Pahlavi, embarked on an ambitious drive aimed at asserting Iran's position as the leading power in the Persian Gulf. To justify this policy, the Shah argued that the responsibility for maintaining Gulf security lay solely with the local states and that no external powers were to be allowed to interfere in the affairs of the region. As the largest and most powerful Gulf country, he believed Iran had a moral, historical and geopolitical obligation to ensure stability in this region not only for regional benefits but also for the good of the world.

The Shah's perception of Iran as the "guardian of the Gulf" manifested itself in an impressive build-up of Iran's military capabilities, as well as a string of Iranian moves intended to signal—both to the Gulf countries and the great powers—exactly who had the final say in the region. One such move was the unilateral abrogation, in April 1969, of Iran's 1937 treaty with Iraq on the navigation rules in the Shatt al-Arab. According to this agreement, the frontier between the two countries had been fixed at the low-water mark on the eastern side of the river. This had given Iraq control over the entire waterway, except for the area near the Iranian towns of Abadan and Khorramshahr where the frontier had been designated at the *thalweg* (the median, deep-water line). Another benefit Iraq derived from the treaty had been the stipulation that ships sailing the Shatt were to have Iraqi pilots and fly the Iraqi flag, except in the area where the frontier was fixed at the *thalweg*.

Now that Iran no longer considered itself bound in any way by the old treaty, it refused to pay tolls to Iraq and to comply with the requirement that all vessels using the Shatt fly the Iraqi flag. In response, Iraq declared that Iran's unilateral abrogation of the 1937 treaty was a blatant violation of international law. Emphasizing that the entire Shatt al-Arab was an integral part of Iraq, and the country's sole access to the Gulf, Baghdad threatened to prevent Iranian vessels from using the waterway unless they abided by the flagging regulations. In complete disregard of the warning, on April 24, 1969, an Iranian merchant ship escorted by the Iranian navy passed through the disputed waters of the Shatt to Iranian ports and paid no toll to Iraq as required by the 1937 treaty. Iraq did not stop the Iranian ship, but before long the two countries were deploying military forces along the Shatt.

No less disturbing for the Iraqi leadership was the extensive military support extended by Iran to the Kurdish separatist struggle, perhaps the thorniest problem of 20th-century Iraq. Not only did Kurdish separatism have the potential to render the Iraqi state non-viable, given the fact that approximately two-thirds of its oil production and oil reserves come from a predominantly Kurdish area, and Kurdistan's fertile lands make it Iraq's main granary, but it also raised the fearful spectre of the possible disintegration of the entire state into three entities: Kurdish, Shi'ite and Sunni.

Because of these weighty considerations the central government in Baghdad had always been adamant on keeping Kurdistan an integral part of Iraq. The Kurds, for their part, sheltered by rugged mountainous terrain, which made military operations in the area extremely difficult, embarked on a sustained struggle against the regime, which has continued with varied intensity to date. As Iran's support for the Kurdish insurgency was growing by the day, a direct Iraqi–Iranian military confrontation ensued in the winter of 1973–1974, which brought the Iraqi army and economy to the verge of collapse.

In these circumstances, the Iraqi regime saw no alternative but to seek some kind of understanding with Iran that would lead to the withdrawal of Iranian support for the Kurds. This took the form of the Algiers Agreement of March 1975, which, at one stroke, terminated the armed confrontation between the two countries, settled the Shatt al-Arab dispute, and paved the way for the suppression of the Kurdish rebellion. According to the agreement, the joint border was to be demarcated in a way that implied, *inter alia*, the renunciation of the Iraqi claim to the Iranian province of Khuzestan (or, as Arabs had been persistent in calling it, "Arabistan"). No less important from the Iranian point of view, the agreement stipulated the delimitation of the river boundaries in the Shatt al-Arab along the old median, deep-water line, thus acknowledging Iran's sovereignty over half of the waterway.

There is little doubt that Iraq made the most concessions in the Algiers Agreement. It paid a high territorial price to secure the inviolability of its frontier, a fundamental and self-evident attribute of statehood, while Iran made no practical concessions (unless non-interference in the domestic affairs of another sovereign state can be so considered). The severity of these concessions is evident in the light of the supreme importance of the Shatt, Iraq's sole access to the Gulf, for Iraqi politico-strategic and economic needs. While Iran has a long Gulf coastline of about 1250 miles (2000 km), Iraq is virtually landlocked, with a Gulf coastline of only 25 miles (40 kilometers). While Iran had five naval bases along the Gulf coast, some of them beyond

Iraq's effective operational reach, Iraq had to rely on two naval bases, Basra and Umm Qasr, both very vulnerable and well within the range of Iranian artillery.

Whatever the balance of concessions, the Algiers Agreement restored a sense of calm to Iraqi–Iranian relations. Having achieved his territorial objectives, the Shah became a *status quo* power advocating the preservation of Gulf stability. Iraq, for its part, was neither able nor inclined to undermine the newly established status. Instead the regime preferred to turn inwards, to concentrate on the defeat of the Kurdish insurgency, the reconstruction of its armed forces and the stabilization of its social, economic and political systems.

Chronology

1979 January 26 Shah Mohammed Reza Pahlavi flees Iran
February Ayatollah Khomeini arrives in Tehran after 15 years of exile. Revolutionary forces take over government
April 1 Islamic Republic of Iran declared
June The revolutionary regime starts urging Iraqis to rise against their rulers
July 16 Saddam Hussein becomes President of Iraq
1980 February 3 Bani Sadr takes office as Iran's first president
March 8 Iran withdraws its ambassador from Iraq
April 1 Iraq's Deputy Premier, Tariq Aziz, escapes an Iranian attempt on his life
April 15 Abortive attempt on the life of Iraq's Minister of Information, Latif Nusseif al-Jasim
May–August Clashes along the border intensify
September 4 Iran shells Khanaqin and Mandali
September 10 Iraq claims to have "liberated" some disputed territory
September 17 Iraq abrogates the 1975 Algiers Agreement and declares it will exercise full sovereignty over the Shatt al-Arab
September 23 Iraqi forces invade Iran
September 28 Iraq halts at the outskirts of Ahvaz and Susangerd; ready to accept a ceasefire

October 5 Iraq seeks ceasefire; rejected by Iran
October 6 Khorramshahr surrounded. Street fighting begins
October 22 Abadan besieged by the Iraqis
October 24 Khorramshahr falls
October 25–26 Iraq fires missiles at Dezful
November 30 Iranian aircraft attack Iraq's nuclear research center at Tuwaitha
December 7 Saddam Hussein announces that Iraq will hold the occupied territories but not advance further, and will resort to a defensive strategy
December 24 First Iraqi air raid on Iran's main oil terminal at Kharg Island
1981 January 5–11 Major Iranian counteroffensive around Susangerd fails
March 19–20 Unsuccessful Iraqi attempt to take Susangerd
May 31 Iranian attack near Qasr-e-Shirin and Dehloran
June 7 Israel destroys Iraq's Osiraq nuclear reactor
June 20 President Bani Sadr removed
June 28 Iraqi offer of a Ramadan ceasefire rejected
September 27–29 Operation Thamin al-Aimma: Iran breaks siege of Abadan
November 5 Iraq offers Muharram ceasefire. Rejected

November 29–December 7 Operation Jerusalem Way: Iran retakes Bostan, threatening to cut off Iraqi forces in Susangerd

December 12–16 Iranian offensive in the Qasr-e-Shirin area

1982 March 22–30 Operation Undeniable Victory: Iranian offensive in Dezful Shush area. Iraqi forces driven back

April 10 Syria closes its oil pipeline to Iraqi oil

April 12 Saddam Hussein announces Iraq will withdraw from Iran if it receives guarantees that this would end the war

April 24–May 25 Operation Jerusalem: Iran occupies most of Khuzestan (May 22–Khorramshahr liberated)

June 10 Iraq announces a ceasefire; rejected by Iran

June 12 UN resolution calls for a ceasefire

June 20 Saddam announces that Iraqi troops will be withdrawn from all Iranian territories within ten days

July 13–August 2 Operation Ramadan: five Iranian offensives to capture Basra. Very small gains but large losses

August 9 Separate ministry for the Revolutionary Guards Corps (Pasdaran) established

October 1–10 Operation Muslim Ibn Aqil: directed against Baghdad and Mandali. Repulsed

November 1–11 Operation Muharram: four Iranian offensives in the Amara area. Made small gains but failed to penetrate deep into Iraq

1983 February 6–16 Operation Before Dawn: Iranian offensive in the southern sector in the Musian area. Failed

April 10–17 Operation Dawn: Iranian offensive in the southern sector near Amara. Failed

May 4 Tudeh Party dissolved in Iran

June 7 Iraq proposes a ceasefire. Offer rejected

July 27 Tariq Aziz announces Iraq will escalate attacks on oil installations in Iran

July 22–30 Operation Dawn 2: Iranian offensive in Kurdistan. Advanced nine miles (14.5 km) inside Iraq and captured the garrison of Hajj Omran

July 30–August 9 Operation Dawn 3: Iranian offensive in the central front in the region of Mehran. Repulsed

October 20–November 21 Operation Dawn 4: Iranian offensive in the northern sector aimed at taking Penjwin. Pushed a few miles into Iraq

November 2 Iraq warns merchant vessels to avoid the "war zone" at the northern end of the Gulf

1984 February "Tanker war" begins

February 7–22 First "war of the cities"

February 15–24 Operations Dawn 5 and 6: largest Iranian offensive in the war to date. A thrust along a 150-mile (240 km) front between Mehran and Bostan

February 24–March 19 Operation Khaibar: series of Iranian thrusts in the direction of Basra. Failed but not before capturing Majnun Island

October 18–25 Operation Dawn 7: limited Iranian offensive on the central front (Mehran)

1985 January 28–early February First Iraqi offensive since 1980 on the central front (Qasr-e-Shirin). Failed

March 11–23 Operation Badr: Iranian offensive in the direction of Basra. Failed

March 22–April 8 Second war of the cities

June Fighting on Majnun Island

July Month-long Iranian operation in Kurdistan

Mid-August–December Iraqi aerial campaign against Kharg Island. Approximately 60 raids

1986 January 6–10 Iraqi attack on Majnun Island

February 9–25 Operation Dawn 8: Iranian offensive on the southern front. Fao Peninsula captured

February 14–March 3 Operation Dawn 9: Iranian offensive in Kurdistan. Drove a few miles from Suleimaniya then pushed back

February 25 UN resolution on a ceasefire

May 12–14 Iraq captures Mehran. Offer to trade it for Fao dismissed by Iran

June 30–July 9 Operation Karbala 1: Iran recaptures Mehran

August 3 Saddam announces a four-point peace plan

August 12 Successful long-range air raid on Iran's oil terminal on Sirri Island (150 miles [240 km] north of the Strait of Hormuz)

August 31 Operation Karbala 2: Iranian offensive in Kurdistan

September 1–23 Operation Karbala 3: Iranian offensive around the Fao Peninsula and Majnun Island

November 25 Air raid on Iran's Larak Island oil terminal

December 24–26 Operation Karbala 4: Iranian offensive in the direction of Basra

1987 **January 9–February 25** Operation Karbala 5: a large Iranian offensive in the direction of Basra. Failed with heavy casualties

January 14–18 Operation Karbala 6: Iranian offensive in the Sumar area

January 17–25 Third war of the cities

February–April Fourth war of the cities

February 12 Iranian Operation Fatah 4 begins in Kurdistan

March 7 Operation Karbala 7: Iranian offensive in the Hajj Omran area in Kurdistan

March 23 US offers to protect Kuwaiti tankers in the Gulf

April 6 Kuwait suggests re-registration of some tankers to US ownership for protection, and seeks transfer of others to Soviet registry

April 6–9 Operation Karbala 8: Iranian offensive in the direction of Basra

April 9 Operation Karbala 9: Iranian offensive in the Qasr-e-Shirin area

April 14 USSR announces it will lease three tankers to Kuwait so as to reduce Iranian attacks on Kuwaiti shipping

April 15 Iran warns Kuwait against leasing tankers to outside powers

May 6 US agrees in principle to re-register 11 Kuwaiti tankers under US flag

July 20 UN Security Council passes Resolution 598 calling for ceasefire and withdrawal of Iranian and Iraqi forces to internationally recognized boundaries. Welcomed by Iraq and rejected by Iran for not naming Iraq as aggressor

July 22 US Navy starts convoying Kuwaiti tankers flying US flag

September 4 Iran fires missile at Kuwait; Kuwait expels 15 Iranian diplomats

September 22 US ship attacks and captures Iranian mine-laying vessel with mines on board

October 8–22 US sinks three Iranian patrol boats in the Gulf; Iran fires missiles at unprotected US-owned tankers; US destroys disused Iranian oil platform; Iraq attacks Kuwaiti oil terminal with Silkworm sea-to-sea missile

1988 **January 14–15** Iran attacks three tankers in two days

February 29–April 30 Fifth war of the cities

March 15–16 Iraqi forces gas the Kurdish town of Halabja, killing thousands of civilians

March 19 First Iranian–Kuwaiti military encounter as Iran attacks Bubian Island

April 18 Iraq recaptures the Fao Peninsula after two days of heavy fighting; American warships sink six Iranian vessels

May 25 Iraq recaptures territory around Salamcheh, held by Iran since January 1987

June 25 Iraq drives Iranian forces from Majnun Island

July 3 USS *Vincennes* shoots down Iranian airliner in the Gulf, mistaking it for a fighter

July 13–17 Iraq pushes into Iranian territory for the first time since 1982, then withdraws its forces and offers peace

July 17 Iran implicitly accepts a ceasefire by unconditionally accepting UN Resolution 598

July 20 Ayatollah Khomeini's acceptance of a ceasefire broadcast on Tehran Radio. Iraq continues the offensive along the border

August 20 Ceasefire begins

August 24 Iranian and Iraqi foreign ministers open peace talks in Geneva

The quest for the empire of God

Slide to war

The status quo achieved by the Algiers Agreement was brought to an abrupt end by the Iranian Revolution of January 1979. It was headed by the radical cleric Ayatollah Ruhollah Khomeini, who had been expelled from Iran by the Shah in 1964 for his opposition to the regime. Khomeini espoused a militant religious doctrine rejecting not only the Middle Eastern political order, but also the contemporary international system since both perpetuated an unjust order imposed on the "oppressed" Muslims by the "oppressive" great powers. It was bound to be replaced by an Islamic world order in which the territorial nation-state would be transcended by the broader entity of the *umma* (or the universal Muslim community); and since Iran was the only

country where the "Government of God" had been established, it had the sacred obligation to serve as the core of the *umma* and a springboard for the worldwide dissemination of Islam's holy message. As he put it: "We will export our revolution throughout the world . . . until the calls 'there is no god but God and Muhammad is the messenger of God' are echoed all over the world."

Khomeini made good his promise. In November 1979 and February 1980, widespread riots erupted in the Shi'ite towns of the oil-rich Saudi province of Hasa, exacting dozens of casualties. Similar disturbances occurred in Bahrain during 1979–80, while Kuwait became the target of a sustained terrorist and subversive campaign. Yet the main thrust of the subversive effort was directed against Iraq. This was for two main

In January 1979, the Shah of Iran, Mohammed Reza Pahlavi, fled the country in the face of a popular revolution. (Gamma)

In February 1979, the exiled Ayatollah Ruhollah Khomeini triumphantly returned to Tehran, after 15 years of forced exile, as founding father of the Islamic Republic of Iran. (Gamma)

reasons. First, Shi'ites accounted for approximately 60 percent of Iraq's total population, and they deeply resented the longstanding discrimination exercised against them by the Sunni minority, less than one-third their size; the revolutionary regime in Tehran could, and certainly did, entertain hopes that this Shi'ite community would emulate the Iranian example and rise against their Sunni "oppressors." Secondly, given Iraq's position as the largest and most powerful Arab state in the Gulf, it was viewed by the revolutionary regime as the main obstacle to Iran's quest for regional hegemony. In the words of the influential member of the Iranian leadership, Hujjat al-Islam Sadeq Khalkhali: "We have taken the path of true Islam and our aim in defeating Saddam Hussein lies in the fact that we consider him the main obstacle to the advance of Islam in the region."

From their early days in power, the clerics in Tehran embarked on a subversive campaign against Iraq's ruling Ba'ath regime and its leader Saddam Hussein. In April 1980, the Iraqi Deputy Prime Minister, Tariq Aziz, narrowly escaped an attempt on his life. (Gamma)

In June 1979, the revolutionary regime began publicly urging the Iraqi population to rise up and overthrow the secular Ba'th regime, which had governed Iraq since the summer of 1968. A few months later Tehran escalated its campaign by resuming support for the Iraqi Kurds (which had been suspended in 1975), providing aid to underground Shi'ite movements in Iraq and initiating terrorist attacks against prominent Iraqi officials. These reached their peak on April 1, 1980, with a failed attempt on the life of the Iraqi Deputy Premier, Tariq Aziz, while he was making a public speech in Baghdad. Two weeks later, the Iraqi Minister of Information, Latif Nusseif al-Jasim, narrowly escaped a similar attempt. In April alone, at least 20 Iraqi officials were killed in bomb attacks by Shi'ite underground organizations.

The militancy of the Iranians stood in sharp contrast to Iraq's appeasing approach. Not only did the ruling Ba'th regime refuse to exploit the revolutionary strife in Iran for political or territorial gains, but it extended a hand of friendship to the new rulers in Tehran: the Iranian Prime Minister, Mehdi Bazargan, was invited to visit Baghdad, Iraq offered its good offices in case Iran decided to join the non-aligned movement, and the revolutionary regime was praised for reinforcing the "deep historical relations" between the two peoples. In a speech on July 17, 1979, shortly after his ascendancy to the presidency, Saddam Hussein reiterated Iraq's desire to establish relations of friendship and co-operation with Iran, based on mutual non-interference in internal affairs.

By the end of 1979, however, little was left of the official optimism with which Iraq had greeted the Iranian Revolution, and the Ba'th leadership moved to contain the Iranian subversive campaign. It suppressed the underground organizations, expelling some 100,000 Iraqi Shi'ites from the country, attempted to organize a united pan-Arab front, and supported separatist Kurdish and Arab elements within Iran. These countermeasures, however, failed to impress the ayatollahs. On March 8, 1980, Iran announced that it was withdrawing its ambassador from Iraq, and by April 7 its remaining diplomatic staff had been ordered home. The following month the Iranian–Iraqi confrontation entered a new and more dangerous phase with clashes along the common border. These escalated in August into heavy fighting, involving tank and artillery duels as well as air strikes.

Iran's subversive activities in general—and the protracted and escalating border fighting in particular—put the Iraqi leadership in an almost impossible position. On the one hand, war at that particular juncture could not be more ill-timed. Due to the world oil boom in 1979 and 1980, the Iraqi economy enjoyed unprecedented prosperity. Oil export revenues rose from $1 billion in 1972 to $21 billion in 1979 and $26 billion in 1980. During the months preceding the war, these revenues were running at an annual rate of $33 billion, enabling the regime to carry out ambitious development programs. Numerous construction projects mushroomed throughout the country. Baghdad was grooming itself to host the summit of the non-aligned movement in 1982. The living conditions of many groups within Iraq were on the rise. War could only risk these achievements and, in consequence, damage the domestic standing of the Ba'th.

Yet, in the face of the growing evidence of Iran's real agenda, the Iraqis became increasingly reluctant to live in the shadow of the Iranian threat. The revolutionary regime in Tehran was nothing like anything they had met before. The Shah, for all his military power and ambitious designs, was viewed as unpleasant but rational. Certainly his goals were opposed to Iraqi national interests, and their satisfaction came necessarily at Iraq's expense. However, he did not seek to remove the Ba'th regime, and was amenable to peaceful co-existence once his objectives had been achieved. The revolutionary regime, on the other hand, was a completely different type of rival—an irrational actor motivated by uncompromising ideology, and by the pursuance of goals that were wholly unacceptable to the Ba'th regime.

To the Iraqi president, Saddam Hussein, this threat seemed particularly ominous. Ascending to power in July 1979, he perceived the world as a violent, hostile place where the ultimate objective of staying alive, and in power, justified all means. This bleak vision of humanity, memorably described some 350 years previously by Thomas Hobbes, drove Saddam to transform Iraq into one of the world's most repressive police states. During his years in power— both as *de facto* leader under President Ahmad Hasan al-Bakr since the early 1970s, and as President—Saddam completely subjected the ruling Ba'th Party to his will, sterilizing its governing institutions and reducing the national decision-making apparatus to one man, surrounded by a docile flock of close associates. Pre-empting any and all dissent through systematic purges (his ascent to the presidency, for example, was accompanied by the elimination of hundreds of party officials and military officers, some of whom were close friends and associates), he subordinated all domestic and foreign policies to one, and only one, goal: his political survival.

Now that the mullahs in Tehran would not relent their sustained assault on his regime, Saddam was gradually driven to the conclusion that the only way to deflect the Iranian threat was to exploit Iran's temporary weakness following the revolution and to raise the stakes for both sides by resorting to overt, state-supported armed force. On September 7, 1980, Iraq accused Iran of shelling Iraqi border towns from territories that, according to the Algiers Agreement, belonged to Iraq, and demanded the immediate evacuation of Iranian forces from these areas. Soon afterwards Iraq moved to "liberate" these disputed territories and, on September 10, announced that the mission had been accomplished. For his part, the Iranian acting Chief-of-Staff announced on September 14 that his country no longer abided by the 1975 Algiers Agreement on the land borders. Saddam responded three days later by abrogating the agreement. From here the road to war was short.

"The frequent and blatant Iranian violations of Iraqi sovereignty have rendered the 1975 Algiers Agreement null and void." Five days after Iraqi President Saddam Hussein unilaterally abrogated the agreement, Iraqi forces invaded Iran. (Gamma)

Strengths and weaknesses of Iran and Iraq

Since the creation of the modern Middle East in the wake of the First World War on the ruins of the Ottoman Empire, Iran has been the pre-eminent power in the Persian Gulf, far superior to Iraq on every quantitative index of power. Iran's territory is three times the size of Iraq's, its population is similarly larger (39 million in 1980, compared with Iraq's 13 million), and its 1,243-mile-long (2,000 km) coastline is 50 times longer than that of Iraq.

Moreover, while neither of the two countries is demographically homogeneous, Iraq's ethnic and religious divisions are far deeper and more intractable than those of Iran. It is a country where the main non-Arab community, the Kurds, has been constantly suppressed, and where the majority of the population, the Shi'ites, has been ruled as an underprivileged class by a minority group, the Sunnis, less than one-third their number. In contrast, the Shi'ites of Iran (about 95 percent of the population) are governed by fellow Shi'ites, while the proportion of Kurds in Iran's population is less than half that of Iraq.

To this must be added Iraq's geopolitical and topographical inferiority to Iran. Not only is Iraq virtually landlocked and surrounded by six neighbors, with at least two—Turkey and Iran—larger and more powerful, but its foremost strategic and economic assets are dangerously close to these two states. The northern oil-rich provinces of Mosul and Kirkuk, accounting for most of Iraq's oil production, lie near the Turkish and Iranian borders, while Baghdad and Basra are only 75 and 19 miles

(120 and 30 km) respectively from the Iranian border. The Shatt al-Arab waterway, Iraq's only outlet to the Gulf, can easily be controlled by Iran. This stands in stark

Since the inception of the modern state of Iraq in 1921, its largest community, the Shi'ites, have been ruled as an underprivileged class by their Sunni counterparts, less than one-third their number. (Rex Features)

contrast to Iran's major strategic centers, which are located deep inside the country (Tehran is some 435 miles [700 km] from the frontier) and enjoy better topographical protection than their Iraqi counterparts.

Building on these intrinsic strengths, during the 1970s the Shah transformed the Iranian military into a formidable force armed with the most advanced Western major weapons systems. By early 1979, the Iranian air force had 447 combat aircraft, including 66 of the highly advanced F-14s, compared with Iraq's 339 less sophisticated aircraft. Iran's naval superiority was even more pronounced. The Iranian navy had seven guided-missile ships (destroyers and frigates), four gun corvettes, six missile-armed fast attack craft (FAC) and 14 hovercraft. The Iraqi navy was a much more modest force of 12 FAC.

The balance of forces on the ground was somewhat more even. While the Iranian

Upon seizing power in Iran, the revolutionary regime embarked on a systematic purge of the Shah's military and security forces. Many were court-martialed and summarily executed. (Gamma)

army was much larger (285,000 against 190,000), the number of combat formations and major weapons systems was about equal: ten (small Soviet-style) Iraqi divisions were organized under three corps headquarters compared with six (larger US-style) Iranian divisions grouped into three field armies. Tank holdings were similar (1,800 Iraqi against 1,735 Iranian) as were artillery pieces (800 Iraqi, 1,000 Iranian). Modelled largely on the Soviet forces, the Iraqi army was relatively strong in all kinds of armored fighting vehicles (AFV).

Yet this apparent equality is quite misleading. The Iranian army's only realistic mission was the security of Iran's western border (since the Soviet military threat was largely discounted, at least from the early 1960s). Iraq's army, on the other hand, had to defend three critical frontiers—the Iranian, the Turkish, and the Syrian—and also to contain the Kurds. In fact, given the implacable hostility between Iraq's and Syria's ruling Ba'th parties, in the late 1970s the Syrian border was more of a security problem than the Iranian. In 1975–76 the two countries came close to war over the distribution of water from the Euphrates and Syria's direct intervention in the Lebanese conflict.

This strategic balance was profoundly reversed by the Islamic Revolution. Viewing the armed forces as the Shah's instrument of oppression and as the most dangerous potential source of counter-revolution, the mullahs established their own militia, the Revolutionary Guards, or Pasdaran, while embarking on a systematic purge of the military. Between February and September 1979, some 85 senior officers were executed and hundreds more (including all major-generals and most brigadier-generals) were imprisoned or forced to retire. By September 1980, some 12,000 officers had been purged.

The purges dealt a devastating blow to the operational capabilities of the Iranian military: the army lost over half its officers in the ranks of major to colonel, while the air force lost half of its pilots and 15–20 percent of its officers, NCOs and technicians. Over and above the purges, about half of the regular servicemen deserted and many more were killed during and after the revolution; conscription was not enforced and some fighting formations were dissolved, including the Imperial Guard, the army's foremost brigade; others fell apart or were much reduced.

By the outbreak of the war, Iran found itself inferior to Iraq: the Iranian army was down from 285,000 to around 150,000, whereas the Iraqi army stood at 200,000. The operational implications of this decrease in Iranian manpower were even more far-reaching. While the Iraqi army had increased its divisions to 12 since the fall of the Shah (by adding two new mechanized divisions), the operational strength of the Iranian army shrank to six understrength divisions, which were probably no more than the equivalent of brigades. Hence, while Iraq could deploy almost all its major weapons systems (2,750 tanks, 2,500 AFV and some 920 artillery pieces), Iran could hardly deploy half of its 1,735 tanks, 1,735 AFV and 1,000 artillery pieces.

The balance of forces in the air was no more favorable to Iran. Apart from the suspension of the Shah's ambitious procurement programs (particularly the plan to buy 160 F-16 fighters), which had been expected to significantly enhance the air force's operational strength, the revolutionary air force suffered from acute maintenance and logistical problems. Key avionics were removed from most of Iran's F-14s with the departure of the American advisers and many of the sensor, maintenance and logistical systems of the F-4s and F-5s were beginning to break down due to a lack of spare parts and proper maintenance. Consequently, by the outbreak of the war, the understrength Iranian air force (70,000 compared to 100,000 in 1979) was able to fly only half its aircraft. The Iraqi air force, on the other hand, had modernized its front line with the introduction of some 140 Su-20 and MiG-23 fighter aircraft and maintained a high level of serviceability (about 80 percent at the start of the war).

Only at sea was Iran's pre-1979 superiority maintained. Even though the navy did not completely escape the purges, and although it suffered from maintenance and logistical problems, Iran's naval superiority had been so pronounced that it could be maintained, regardless of the deterioration in the navy's operational strength.

But numbers do not tell the whole story. The quality of military leadership, combat experience, training, and command and control also count. And in this respect, both armed forces had little to show for themselves. Both were commanded by politicized and tightly controlled leaderships, where loyalty to the regime was a prerequisite for promotion, where critical thinking was tantamount to subversion, and where religious and social affiliations were far more important than professionalism.

Never forgetting the involvement of military officers in the 1953 attempt to force him from his throne, the Shah took great pains to keep the three services well apart so that they were incapable of mounting a coup or undermining his regime. There was no joint chiefs-of-staff organization, nor were the three services linked in any way except through the Shah, who was the Commander-in-Chief. Every officer above the rank of colonel (or equivalent) was personally appointed by the Shah, and all flying cadets were vetted by him. Finally, he used four different intelligence services to maintain surveillance of the officer corps.

These precautionary measures were mirrored on the Iraqi side. Keenly aware that in non-democratic societies force constituted the main agent of political change, Saddam spared no effort to ensure the loyalty of the military to his personal rule. Scores of party commissars had been deployed within the armed forces down to the battalion level. Organized political activity had been banned; "unreliable" elements had been forced to retire, or else purged and often executed; senior officers had constantly been reshuffled to prevent the creation of power bases. The social composition of the Republican Guard, the regime's praetorian guard, had been fundamentally transformed to draw heavily on conscripts from Saddam's home town of Tikrit and the surrounding region.

Saddam also sought to counterbalance the military through a significant expansion of the Ba'th's militia, the Popular Army. Within a year of his seizure of power in 1979, the Popular Army was more than doubled—from 100,000 to 250,000 men. During the Iran–Iraq War it was to become an ominous force some one million strong, using heavy weaponry and participating in some of the war operations. And while this by no means put the Popular Army on a par with the professional military, by denying the latter a monopoly over the state's means of violence, it widened the regime's security margins against potential coups.

Thus, like the Shah, Saddam created a docile and highly politicized military leadership, vetted and promoted on the principle of personal loyalty and kinship rather than professional excellence.

The rapid expansion and modernization of the Iranian and the Iraqi armed forces also had a detrimental impact on their operational competence. Each found it extremely difficult to train, expand and modernize simultaneously. The problems were made worse by the poor quality of conscripts in both countries, for whom the rapid absorption of advanced weapons was extraordinarily difficult. Consequently, despite the massive advisory assistance provided by the arms suppliers (mainly the United States and the Soviet Union), both countries were more or less incapable of maintaining their advanced major weapons systems.

Moreover, both Iranian and Iraqi forces had poor combat experience. In the case of Iran this was limited to the participation of six brigades, along with elements of the navy and the air force, in the suppression of a Marxist rebellion in Oman between 1972 and 1975. Even this was more of a show of force than real combat since the rebels had never numbered more than 2,000, with perhaps no more than 1,000 inside Oman at any given time. Also, the Shah's determination to give combat experience to as many of his units as possible led to their rotation in Oman on a three-month basis, too short a tour of duty to be really useful.

On the face of it, the Iraqi armed forces seemed to have had more combat experience. Not only did they take part in the October 1973 War against Israel, but they had fought a counter-insurgency campaign in Kurdistan for more than a decade. However, the tactics employed during the Kurdish campaign were hardly applicable to a conventional war, and indeed the preoccupation with the Kurdish insurgency affected regular training programs and thus operational capabilities. Nor was Iraq's combat experience in the October War any more impressive: the armored division that arrived at the Golan front ten days after the war began was ambushed by Israeli forces and lost some 100 tanks within a few hours.

In the field of command and control, it did seem that Iraq had an edge at the outbreak of the war, as Saddam, in his capacity as Commander-in-Chief of the armed forces, controlled the war from the Revolutionary Command Council (RCC), where each of the three services was represented. Iran had no joint staff. Abol Hassan Bani Sadr, the Iranian President and Commander-in-Chief, tried to strengthen the central command structure, but his efforts were frustrated to a great extent by the power struggle between the Pasdaran and the armed forces. Consequently, at the outbreak of war, Iran had no central command-and-control system that could co-ordinate the execution of its war strategy.

In qualitative terms, therefore, both armed forces could be judged to be more or less equal. They suffered from similar problems of military leadership caused by the process of selection and promotion; they were both poorly trained; and both had low technical ability to maintain and use their modern weapons. Their combat experience was very limited and they were saddled with inefficient command-and-control systems. Against this background of rough qualitative equality, Iraq's quantitative superiority became all the more significant. Recognizing the temporary nature of this superiority, owing to Iran's fundamental prowess, the Iraqi leadership hurried to take advantage of this unique window of opportunity to pre-empt and frustrate the recovery of the Iranian armed forces from their post-revolutionary débâcle.

Invasion and after

On September 17, 1980, Saddam Hussein addressed his newly re-instated parliament. "The frequent and blatant Iranian violations of Iraqi sovereignty," he said, "have rendered the 1975 Algiers Agreement null and void." Both legally and politically the treaty was indivisible. Once its spirit had been violated, Iraq saw no alternative but to restore the legal position of the Shatt al-Arab to the pre-1975 status. "This river," he continued to enthusiastic applause, "must have its Iraqi–Arab identity restored as it was throughout history in name and in reality with all the disposal rights emanating from full sovereignty over the river."

The implications of this speech were not long in coming. On September 22, emulating the brilliant Israeli gambit of the Six Day War in 1967, Iraqi aircraft pounded ten airfields in Iran in an attempt to destroy the Iranian air force on the ground. This failed, but the next day Iraqi forces crossed the border in strength and advanced into Iran in three simultaneous thrusts along a front of some 400 miles (644 km).

The main effort, involving four of the six invading divisions, was directed against the southern province of Khuzestan, and aimed at separating the Shatt al-Arab from the rest of Iran and establishing a territorial security zone along the southern frontier. Within this framework, two divisions (one armored and one mechanized) looped southwards and laid siege to the strategic towns of Khorramshahr and Abadan, while another two armored divisions left the Iraqi towns of Basra and Amara and in an enveloping movement secured the territory bounded by the line Khorramshahr–Ahvaz–Susangerd–Musian.

The operations on the central and the northern fronts were essentially secondary and supportive efforts, designed to secure

An Iranian refugee with his personal belongings, fleeing the Iraqi invasion. (Gamma)

Iraq against an Iranian counterattack. On the central front, the invading forces occupied the town of Mehran and advanced further east to the foothills of the Zagros Mountains to secure the important road network linking Dezful with northern Iran west of the Zagros and simultaneously block access to Iraq from that direction. Another thrust, further north, secured the critical terrain forward of Qasr-e-Shirin, thus blocking the traditional

Tehran–Baghdad invasion route. A subsidiary attack in the far north, near Penjwin, attempted to establish strong defense positions opposite Suleimaniya, to protect the Kirkuk oil complex.

The invading forces encountered no co-ordinated resistance, as the Iranian military and the Pasdaran conducted their war operations separately, reporting to separate leaderships. Though not taken by

The destruction of Iran's oil refinery in Abadan dealt a
heavy blow to its oil-exporting capabilities. (Gamma)

surface, the army had been unable to complete its war preparations and, as a result, had only one armored division in the whole of Khuzestan, with the majority of its units deployed in the hinterland and the north (along the Soviet border and in Kurdistan). In retrospect, this deployment turned out to be invaluable in that it spared the army heavy casualties and allowed it to preserve its strength and to move on to the offensive.

The Pasdaran, a revolutionary militia established by the Islamic regime as a counterbalance to the professional military, bore the main brunt of the Iraqi invasion. Here, a revolutionary guard using a motorcycle to locate and destroy Iraqi tanks. (Rex Features)

But this would seem to be the wisdom of hindsight; in the short term, Iran's total lack of co-ordination prevented it from putting up an effective defense, leaving the Pasdaran to bear the brunt of the Iraqi assault. Though

The Iraqi invasion of Iran, 1980

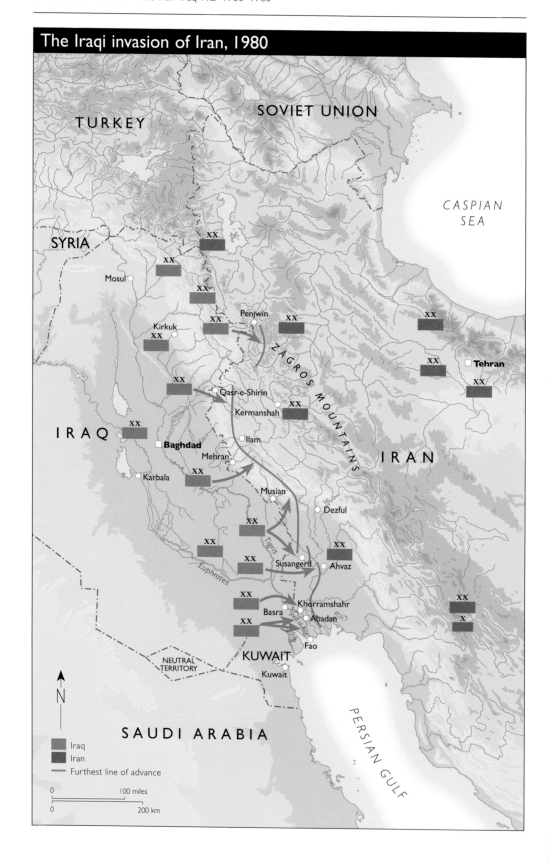

TURKEY

SOVIET UNION

SYRIA

CASPIAN
SEA

Mosul

XX

XX

XX

Penjwin

XX

Kirkuk
XX

XX

ZAGROS

XX

XX
Qasr-e-Shirin

XX

Tehran

XX

IRAQ

XX

Kermanshah

XX

M
O
U
N
T
A
I
N
S

IRAN

Baghdad

Ilam

Mehran

Karbala

XX

Musian

Tigris

Dezful

XX

XX

XX

Euphrates

Susangerd

Ahvaz

XX

XX

XX

XX

XX

XX

Khorramshahr
Basra   Abadan

XX
X

XX

Fao

NEUTRAL
TERRITORY

KUWAIT

Kuwait

N

SAUDI ARABIA

PERSIAN
GULF

■ Iraq
■ Iran
— Furthest line of advance

0   100 miles

0   200 km

poorly trained and ill-equipped (they were armed with light infantry weapons and Molotov cocktails), the Pasdaran fought with the great fervor and tenacity that were to become their trademark, making the Iraqis pay a heavy price in built-up areas. A particularly ferocious battle raged in Khorramshahr, attacked by the Iraqis in early October. Each side suffered about 7,000 dead and seriously wounded, while the Iraqis also lost over 100 tanks and armored vehicles. By the time the whole of Khorramshahr was in Iraqi hands, on October 24, it had come to be referred to by both combatants as "Khunistan," meaning "city of blood."

Nevertheless, what saved Iran from a comprehensive defeat was not the ferocity of its military resistance but rather the limited objectives of the Iraqi invasion. Saddam's decision to go to war was not taken easily or enthusiastically. He did not embark on war in pursuit of a premeditated "grand design" but was pushed into it by his increasing anxiety about the threat to his own political survival. War was not his first choice but rather an act of last resort, adopted only after trying all other means for deflecting Iran's pressure. It was a pre-emptive move, designed to exploit a temporary window of opportunity in order to forestall the Iranian threat to his regime. If Saddam entertained hopes or aspirations beyond the containment of the Iranian danger—as he may have done—these were not the reasons for launching the war but were incidental to it.

The reluctant nature of Saddam's decision to invade Iran was clearly reflected in his war strategy. Instead of attempting to deal a mortal blow to the Iranian army and trying to topple the revolutionary regime in Tehran, he sought to confine the war by restricting his army's goals, means and targets. The invasion was carried out by half of the Iraqi army—six of 12 divisions. Saddam's initial strategy also avoided targets of civilian and economic value in favour of attacks almost exclusively on military targets. Only after the Iranians struck non-military targets did the Iraqis respond in kind.

Nor did Saddam's territorial aims go beyond the Shatt al-Arab and a small portion of the southern region of Khuzestan, where, he hoped, the substantial Arab minority would rise against their Iranian "oppressors." This did not happen. The underground Arab organization in Khuzestan proved to be a far cry from the mass movement anticipated by the Iraqis, and the Arab masses remained conspicuously indifferent to their would-be liberators.

Saddam hoped that a quick, limited, yet decisive, campaign would convince Iran's revolutionary regime to desist from its attempts to overthrow him. By exercising self-restraint, he sought to signal his defensive aims and an intent to avoid all-out war with the hope that Tehran would respond in kind, and perhaps even be willing to reach a settlement. In the words of the Iraqi Foreign Minister, Tariq Aziz, "Our military strategy reflects our political objectives. We want neither to destroy Iran nor to occupy it permanently because that country is a neighbor with which we will remain linked by geographical and historical bonds and common interests. Therefore we are determined to avoid any irrevocable steps."

Apart from these overriding political considerations, Saddam's strategy of limited war reflected a keen awareness of Iraq's geographical constraints. On the one hand, Iran's strategic depth and the distance of its major centers from the border constituted a formidable operational and logistical obstacle to a general war. On the other, Iran's huge hinterland and the remoteness of the bulk of its forces from the frontier allowed Saddam to secure his limited objectives before the Iranian army could concentrate against his forces, or before the onset of the winter rains in November, which could make off-road traffic in most parts of Iran extremely difficult.

Moreover, the nature of the terrain also militated in the direction of a swift and limited campaign, in that it was more favorable to the defender. The Shatt al-Arab waterway and the broad expanses of marshland and waterways hampered vehicle traffic and thus considerably increased the logistical problems faced by the Iraqi invasion forces. Indeed, Iraq's relative success in crossing the numerous water obstacles in Khuzestan in the initial stage of the war resulted mainly from the lack of an organized Iranian defense. Yet once given the necessary breathing space, Iran quickly exploited the advantages offered by the terrain by flooding certain areas to deny their use to Iraqi forces.

This mixture of political and geographical considerations compounded Saddam's failure to grasp the operational requirements of such a campaign. Rather than allowing his forces to advance until their momentum was exhausted, he voluntarily halted their advance within a week of the onset of hostilities and then announced his willingness to negotiate a settlement. This decision not to capitalize on Iraq's early military successes by applying increased

pressure had a number of dire consequences which, in turn, led to the reversal of the course of the war. It saved the Iranian army from a decisive defeat and gave Tehran precious time to re-organize and regroup; and it had a devastating impact on the morale of the Iraqi army and hence on its combat performance. Above all, the limited Iraqi invasion did nothing to endanger the revolutionary regime, nor to drive Ayatollah Khomeini towards moderation.

Most governments, of course, would react strongly to a foreign armed intervention, but a revolutionary regime under attack is all the more likely to respond with vehemence when it has not yet gained full legitimacy and still has many internal enemies. Like the French almost two centuries earlier, the Iranians channeled national (and religious) fervor into resisting an external threat. Instead of seeking a quick accommodation, the clerics in Tehran capitalized on the Iraqi attack to consolidate their regime, diminish the power struggle within their own ranks and suppress opposition to their rule. As early as September 24, the Iranian navy attacked Basra and, on the way, destroyed two oil terminals near the port of Fao, thereby severely reducing Iraq's oil-exporting capacity. The Iranian air force struck at a variety of strategic targets within Iraq, including oil facilities, dams, petrochemical plants and the nuclear reactor near Baghdad. By October 1, Baghdad itself had been subjected to eight air raids. Iraq retaliated with a series of strikes against Iranian targets, and the two sides quickly became interlocked in widespread strategic exchanges.

Perhaps in recognition of his mistake, in late October to early November 1980, Saddam attempted to reverse the tide of events by striking in the direction of Dezful and Ahvaz, only to discover that it was too little too late. Had the two cities been attacked in September, Iranian resistance might well have crumbled. By November, with these sites transformed into military strongholds, and in the face of heavy winter rains, Iraq found their occupation unattainable. As a result, Saddam had to pay a far higher price for a limited invasion than he had anticipated.

The Iraqi invasion allowed Iran's revolutionary regime to consolidate its power and rally the nation behind its war effort. (Gamma)

The delicate balance of incompetence

With the fall of Khorramshahr on October 24, 1980, the two combatants settled for static warfare, which was to continue for some eight months. Having swept aside the Pasdaran and occupied the territories assigned as the objectives, Iraq seemed quite satisfied with its strategic position and showed no appetite for further territorial gains. On December 7 Saddam announced that Iraq had reverted to a defensive strategy and would attempt no further advances. Iran, for its part, beset by domestic instability and busy regrouping its forces, was not yet prepared to move on to the offensive. Fighting was consequently reduced to mutual artillery exchanges and air raids, especially against strategic targets, with ground operations limited to sporadic sabotage raids by Iraqi and Iranian forces.

With the halt of the Iraqi invasion in October 1980, fighting was reduced to artillery exchanges and air raids against strategic targets. (Gamma)

Abol Hassan Bani Sadr, Iraq's President and Commander-in-Chief at the start of the war, was sacked from his post in June 1981 due to unbridgeable differences with the clerics. (Gamma)

There were a number of deviations from this pattern. At the end of December, Iraqi forces advanced in the vicinity of Penjwin to provide better protection for the Kirkuk oil fields, incapacitated by a string of Iranian air strikes, and to support Kurdish guerrillas operating in northern Iran at the time. For its part Iran made one significant attempt to break the stalemate: on January 5, 1981, an armored division broke out of Susangerd and crossed the Karkheh River to the west in an attempt to breach the Iraqi lines. This counteroffensive was initially successful and managed to penetrate deep into Iraqi lines. But success was shortlived: the Iraqi line strained but held. Within a few days Iraqi forces managed to envelop the advancing Iranian division and almost annihilate it in one of the largest tank battles of the war. The Iranian losses in the abortive offensive were heavy: approximately 100 M-60 and Chieftain tanks destroyed and 150 captured. Iraq lost some 50 T-62 tanks.

Both belligerents exploited the period of static war to re-organize and rebuild their forces. Drawing on its bitter experience in the battle for Khorramshahr, Iraq concentrated on establishing new infantry units and tried also to provide its forces encamped in Iran with an adequate long-stay logistical infrastructure. This included the construction of a paved highway from Basra to the front lines near Ahvaz, necessary for keeping the forces there

resupplied during the winter, and of a network of earthen walls along the front to protect against the flooding of the Karun and other rivers.

For its part, Iran used the lull in the fighting to improve its defensive system by flooding certain areas so as to deny their use to Iraqi troops. The purge of the army was peremptorily stopped and reservists were called to duty; intensive training programs (especially for tank crews and maintenance personnel) were initiated, and the army was regrouped and redeployed in the theater. Large numbers of Pasdaran were mobilized and a youth volunteer force, the *Basij e-Mustazafin* (Mobilization of the Deprived), was established. By way of overcoming the lack of operational

BELOW and RIGHT In the spring of 1981 Iran moved to the offensive and in a series of large-scale operations drove the Iraqi forces from its territory. Here Iranian troops on their way to battle during Operation Jerusalem Way, and celebrating the capture of an Iraqi position. (Gamma/Rex Features)

co-ordination revealed in the early phase of the war, when the army and the Pasdaran had adamantly refused to co-operate with each other, a seven-man Supreme Defense Council was established to run the war. Headed by President Bani Sadr, it comprised three members of the professional military and three senior mullahs, one of them acting as Khomeini's personal representative.

Iran counterattacks

The Iranian measures bore the desired fruit. By the spring of 1981 the army had managed to re-organize and regroup, to establish a working relationship, however fragile, with the Pasdaran, and to move on to the offensive. In a prolonged and sustained effort, planned and carried out under the leadership of the army, and combining conventional warfare with the revolutionary zeal of the Pasdaran and the Basij, Iran managed to drive Iraqi forces from its territory.

In May the Iranians managed to dislodge Iraqi forces from the heights controlling Susangerd and to secure the approaches to the city. This victory was followed in late September 1981 by yet another Iranian offensive, this time in Abadan. Though Iraq had expected the offensive for some time, it was nevertheless taken by tactical surprise as a result of diversionary Iranian attacks in various parts of Khuzestan, which led it to redeploy some forces away from Abadan. After three days of heavy fighting, from September 27 to 29, the Iranian forces (two infantry divisions and Pasdaran units with armored and artillery support) succeeded in pushing an Iraqi armored division back across the Karun River, thus lifting the siege of Abadan.

Iranian women help the war effort. (Gamma)

These setbacks had a devastating impact on Iraqi morale. Finding themselves entrenched for months in hastily prepared defense positions, subjected to the hardships of the Iranian winter and the heat of the summer, the Iraqi troops began to lose all sense of purpose. This lack of will, which was reflected in reports of discipline problems and a growing number of desertions, was quickly exploited by Iran for yet another major offensive. Lasting from November 29 to December 7, Operation Jerusalem Way involved fierce fighting amid mud and rain, with seven Pasdaran brigades and three regular brigades against a defending Iraqi division. When the fighting was over, Iran had retaken the town of Bostan and forced the Iraqis to retreat and redeploy.

Operation Jerusalem Way had a number of important operational implications. Straining Iran's planning, operational and command-and-control skills to their utmost, it reflected an improved capability to

Anxious to stem the mounting tide of Iranian successes, Baghdad quickly sued for peace. In February 1982 Taha Yasin Ramadan, Iraq's first Deputy Prime Minister and one of Saddam's closest associates, declared that Iraq was prepared to withdraw from Iran in stages before the conclusion of a peace agreement, once negotiations had begun "directly or through other parties" and showed satisfactory signs of progress. A couple of months later Saddam in person further lowered Iraq's conditions for peace by stating his readiness to pull out of Iran, provided that Iraq was given sufficient assurances that such a move would lead to a negotiated settlement. The scornful Iranian response came in the form of a series of large-scale offensives that practically drove the Iraqi forces out of Iran.

The first of these offensives, Operation Undeniable Victory, started on March 22, 1982, in the Dezful Shush area and lasted approximately a week. It was the largest campaign in the war until then and involved more than 100,000 troops on each side. Iran sent into battle the equivalent of four regular divisions (some 40,000–50,000 troops), about 40,000 Pasdaran, and some 30,000 Basij. The Iraqi forces were made up of the newly formed Fourth Army Corps, consisting of eight divisions, together with some independent brigades and specialized units; of these, three divisions were holding Khorramshahr, and at least another three were defending the Khorramshahr–Ahvaz railway line. Both sides conducted combined-arms operations that made effective use of infantry, artillery, armor and close air support. Because of its decreasing number of front-line aircraft (70–90 operational in mid-1982), Iran relied on attack helicopters for most close air support missions, while Iraq employed strike aircraft, flying more than 150 sorties per day.

Commanded by the young and energetic Chief-of-Staff, General Sayed Shirazi, the Iranian offensive began with a surprise night attack by armored units, followed up with suicidal human-wave assaults by Pasdaran brigades of some 1,000 fighters each.

organize and control large-scale and complex military operations. The counteroffensive also witnessed the first successful use of the "human-wave" tactics that would come to dominate the battlefield, as the ecstatic Pasdaran stormed the heavily fortified Iraqi positions without any artillery or air support. Finally, the occupation of Bostan and its environs increased Iraq's logistics problems. With the road between Amara and the front now under full Iranian control, Iraq was compelled to resupply its forces in the Ahvaz area from the far south.

Following each other in rapid succession, with a view to exhausting the enemy's ammunition, these brigades managed to keep their momentum and to overwhelm the Iraqi positions in the face of heavy casualties. Incited by fiery rhetoric from mullahs, who often led the assaults on the Iraqi positions, second-echelon brigades were spoiling for a fight and could hardly wait to replace weakened or decimated front-line units.

In glaring contrast to these daring tactics, Saddam adopted a highly circumspect approach, ordering his forces to hold on to their positions and attempt neither to move forward nor to withdraw; the most he was prepared to authorize was a local counterattack with an armored division— which was readily repulsed by the Iranians. It was only after five or six days of fighting that Saddam realized the full extent of the danger to his forces and ordered a hasty retreat. But this was too little too late: by now the Iranians had managed to encircle and destroy two Iraqi divisions, taking in the process 15,000–20,000 prisoners and seizing large quantities of weaponry, including some 400 tanks.

The final nail in the coffin of the Iraqi invasion was driven during April–May 1982 by Operation Jerusalem and the recapture of Khorramshahr, whose fall at the beginning of the war had been the high point of the Iraqi invasion. Involving some 70,000 troops, mostly Pasdaran, within flexible battle plans that combined classical maneuvers with guerrilla-type tactics, the operation consisted of two consecutive attacks on the Iraqi strongholds in Khuzestan. The first, which lasted from April 24 to May 12, succeeded in driving Iraqi forces out of the Ahvaz–Susangerd area and secured a bridgehead on the west bank of the Karun River. After two weeks of bitter fighting, and in the face of possible encirclement, Iraqi troops withdrew from the Ahvaz–Susangerd area and redeployed near Khorramshahr, anticipating an Iranian attack on that city. This was not long in coming. Having consolidated their positions

and repulsed a large-scale Iraqi counteroffensive on May 20, the Iranians began an all-out assault on Khorramshahr. After two days of fighting, the panic-stricken Iraqis fled in large numbers, leaving behind a substantial amount of military equipment and some 12,000 of their own troops to become prisoners of war.

Into Iraq

In one of his wisest strategic moves during the war, Saddam decided to bow to the inevitable, to withdraw from Iranian territory still under Iraqi control and to deploy for a static defense along the international border. He reckoned that his demoralized and afflicted army was incapable of maintaining its position in Iran, and that the only conceivable way of containing the Iranian threat was through a formidable line of defense on Iraqi territory along the border. Using the Israeli invasion of Lebanon on June 6, 1982, as a pretext, he offered Iran the chance to stop fighting and to send their troops to the Palestinians' aid, and on June 20 he announced that his troops had started withdrawal from Iran and would complete it within ten days. This move, however, failed to appease the clerics in Tehran. Flushed with their newly won successes, they dismissed the Iraqi initiative out of hand and escalated their declared war aims to include not only the overthrow of the Iraqi leadership but also $US 150 billion in reparations and the repatriation of some 100,000 Shi'ites expelled from Iraq before the outbreak of the war.

Since it is doubtful whether anybody in Tehran seriously believed that Iraq would accept these draconian conditions, the hardening of the Iranian line presaged a shift of the war into Iraqi territory. On June 21, a day after Saddam's peace proposal, Khomeini indicated that an invasion of Iraq was imminent, and the following day Chief-of-Staff Shirazi vowed to "continue the war until Saddam Hussein is overthrown so that we can pray at [the holy Shi'ite town of]

Karbala and Jerusalem." On July 13 a large-scale offensive was launched in the direction of Basra, the second most important city in Iraq.

This time, however, Iran was unpleasantly surprised, as the offensive encountered a solid, well-entrenched Iraqi defense. Having recognized the precarious Iraqi position, as early as the autumn of 1981 Saddam had started to prepare his army for the eventuality of an Iranian invasion of Iraq. The size of the Iraqi army was more than doubled—from 200,000 (12 divisions and three independent brigades) in the summer of 1980 to some 500,000 (23 divisions and nine brigades) by 1985—and an extensive defense system was built along the frontier, behind which the bulk of the Iraqi army was deployed. Approximately eight divisions (the Third Army Corps) were deployed in the southern sector to defend Basra; the Second Army Corps, comprising about 100,000 troops in ten divisions, was deployed on the central front to forestall Iranian attacks in the direction of Baghdad;

the northern front was the responsibility of the First Army Corps (two divisions). The Fourth Army Corps was used as a strategic reserve.

Iraq's preparations proved rewarding: five consecutive human-wave assaults in the direction of Basra in the summer of 1982, involving some 100,000 men, failed to breach the Iraqi defense and were repulsed with heavy losses. A particularly onerous human toll was paid by the Basij, who were used as canon fodder, moving through the Iraqi minefields without any minesweeping equipment so as to clear them for the advancing Pasdaran brigades.

These offensives also saw the first use of gas by Iraq, albeit in an extremely circumspect fashion: it did not go beyond the employment of non-lethal tear gas in a small segment of the battlefield, and Iraq resorted to this action only after warning the Iranians in advance. Yet the success of this experiment (the gas reportedly frustrated the

Praying before battle. (Gamma)

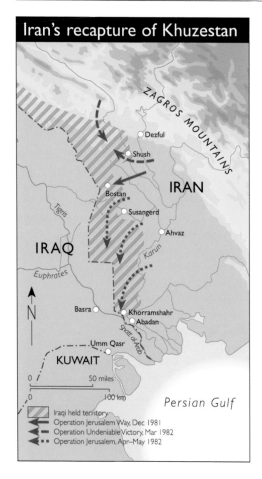

Iran's recapture of Khuzestan

ZAGROS MOUNTAINS

Dezful

Shush

Bostan

IRAN

Susangerd

Ahvaz

Karun

IRAQ

Tigris

Euphrates

N

Basra

Khorramshahr

Abadan

Shatt al-Arab

Umm Qasr

KUWAIT

0   50 miles

0   100 km

Persian Gulf

Iraqi held territory
Operation Jerusalem Way, Dec 1981
Operation Undeniable Victory, Mar 1982
Operation Jerusalem, Apr–May 1982

operations of an entire Iranian division) served to encourage future Iraqi use of chemical weapons.

The failure of the summer 1982 offensive kindled a heated debate within the Iranian leadership about the prudence of invading Iraq. Fearing that such a move would dangerously overextend Iran's military capabilities, the army voiced its opposition to the continued invasion, with Shirazi reportedly threatening to resign if "unqualified people continue to meddle with the conduct of the war." The military was supported by a number of prominent moderate politicians, notably President Ali Khameini, Prime Minister Mir Hossein Mussavi, and Foreign Minister Ali Akbar Velayati, who opposed the invasion on the grounds of its exorbitant human, material and political costs. They were confronted by a powerful hardline group, including the mullahs on the Supreme Defense Council, headed by the influential Speaker of the parliament, Ali Akbar Hashemi-Rafsanjani,

Iran's liberation of Khorramshahr in May 1982 drove the final nail in the coffin of the Iraqi invasion. Some 12,000 Iraqis became prisoners of war. (Gamma)

who urged the acceleration of the military operations at all costs, so as to prevent the Arab world and the international community from rallying behind Iraq.

Though the hardliners eventually won the upper hand, with two large-scale offensives launched in the autumn of 1982 in the direction of Baghdad, theirs was a Pyrrhic victory. The Iranian forces proved unequal to the task. Many experienced men who had volunteered "to save the country" returned to civilian life once Iraqi forces were driven out. More seriously, the decision to invade Iraq undermined the fragile basis of co-operation between the military and the Pasdaran.

Never satisfied with its subordination to the army in the wake of the Iraqi invasion, the Pasdaran persistently strove to disinherit the army from its pre-eminence in the conduct of the war. They were supported in this goal by the mullahs, who wished to see the Pasdaran transformed into Iran's foremost military force that would eventually absorb the regular army. An important step in this direction was made in November 1982, when the Iranian parliament approved the formation of a new Pasdaran ministry. Seizing responsibility from the ministry of defense for the control, deployment and employment of Pasdaran units, the new ministry quickly turned this force into the backbone of the Iranian thrusts into Iraq, with the regular army reducing its participation to the lowest possible level. As the ministry of defense retained responsibility for the overall conduct of the war, the creation of the new Pasdaran ministry effectively institutionalized a reality of two distinct armies, whereby the Pasdaran and the military operated separately without co-ordination or co-operation.

This fragmentation was further exacerbated by the coming of age of the Basij and its development into a substantial force. On March 20, 1982, on the occasion of the Iranian new year, Khomeini announced that "as a special favor" schoolboys between the ages of 12 and 18 years would be allowed to join the Basij and to fight for their country.

Consequently scores of youths volunteered for action and were hastily recruited and provided with "Passports to Paradise," as the admission forms were called. They were then given rudimentary military training, of a week or so, by the Pasdaran, and sent to the front where many of them "martyred" themselves.

Instead of combined-arms operations, which stood at the root of its 1981 operational successes, Iran thus came to rely solely on frontal assaults by large numbers of

The deployment of the Iraqi army after its withdrawal from Iran

poorly trained and ill-equipped militia troops, without adequate armor, artillery, and aerial back-up. As a result, nearly all the Iranian offensives into Iraq were repulsed with heavy casualties.

By the autumn of 1982, then, the war strategies of the two belligerents had undergone a full circle. In the early days of the war, the Iranian Chief-of-Staff, General Valiollah Fallahi (killed in an airplane crash in September 1981), announced that Iran was "essentially fighting a stationary war from dug-in positions, to make it very expensive for the Iraqis to mount offensives." Some 18 months later, Iran was attempting to achieve a decisive victory through mobile operations while Iraq stuck to static defense. Iran now sought to limit the fighting to the battlefield while Iraq took advantage of the deteriorating strength of the Iranian air force to intensify its attacks on a wide range of civilian and economic

Having driven the Iraqi forces from their territory, in July 1982, the Iranians launched a series of incursions into Iraq. These increasingly became dominated by frontal assaults of ill-equipped Pasdaran forces on the heavily fortified Iraqi positions, without adequate artillery or air support. (Gamma)

targets, including ports, industrial facilities, and oil installations.

During 1983, Iran launched five large-scale offensives at different sectors of the front, all of which failed to breach the Iraqi line and were repulsed with heavy losses. Though reflecting a measure of reconstituted co-operation between the army and the Pasdaran, the Iranian tactics remained uninspired: massed frontal infantry attacks on the Iraqi lines, without proper armored, artillery or air support. Iraq, on the other hand, demonstrated more than adequate defensive capabilities, carrying out its operations in an orderly way and taking full advantage of artillery and air supremacy. Moreover, in its first real initiative for nearly a year, Iraq launched a number of local armored counterattacks to frustrate the Iranian offensives, one of them even driving into Iran.

To Saddam's growing exasperation, the repeated Iranian setbacks failed to deflect the regime's readiness to prosecute the war. Quite the reverse, in fact. Rejecting several Iraqi calls for an end to hostilities, in early 1984 the mullahs reiterated their determination to overthrow the Ba'th

Iranian president Ali Khameini was one of the main opponents of Khomeini's decision to extend the war operations into Iraqi territory. (Gamma)

regime. By way of forestalling the Iranian offensives, Iraq augmented its forces along the frontier and designated 11 Iranian cities to be attacked in the event of an Iranian aggression.

Iran remained unimpressed, and on February 7, 1984, the day on which the Iraqi ultimatum expired, launched a probing attack in the northern front. This left Iraq no choice but to carry out the promised attacks on Iranian cities. With the Iranians responding in kind, the two sides were soon engaged in what came to be known as the "first war of the cities" (there would be five such wars before the end of the war).

As things were, not only did this escalation go well beyond Iraq's original intentions (as evidenced by the suspension of air attacks on February 22), but it failed to achieve its major goal, namely the prevention of the anticipated Iranian offensive. On February 15, 1984, the Iranian "final blow" was launched in the central sector.

The offensive was the largest engagement in the war until then, with some 500,000 men under arms pitted against each other along a 150-mile front. Though planned and organized by the regular army staff, it was carried out mainly by the Pasdaran and the Basij, with the army playing a relatively minor role (four to five divisions or approximately 60,000 men out of 250,000 engaged).

The offensive consisted of two stages. The first, operations Dawn 5 (February 15–22) and Dawn 6 (February 22–24), sought to capture the key town of Kut al-Amara and to

Soldiers under fire. (Gamma)

cut the highway linking Baghdad and Basra. After a week of heavy fighting, Iranian forces managed to seize some strategic high ground, about 15 miles (24 km) from the Baghdad–Basra road. Having advanced that far, on February 24 they moved to the second, and more important, stage of the offensive, Operation Khaibar, a series of thrusts in the direction of Basra, which lasted until March 19. For some time it seemed as if the Iranians were about to breach Iraq's formidable line of defense, as they managed to cross the vast expanse of marshland, considered impassable by the Iraqis, and to capture Majnun Island, strategically situated on the southern front, some 40 miles (64 km) north of Basra. They were eventually contained with great effort and brutality, and through the use of chemical weapons (mustard gas and Sarin nerve gas), but managed to retain Majnun Island despite successive Iraqi attempts to dislodge them. Many Iranians jumped into the water to escape the Iraqi firepower, only to be hunted by helicopter gunships and to be electrocuted by electrodes, fitted in some

water channels. Over 3,000 Iranian dead, some very young, were bulldozed into a mass grave, making a distinct ridge in the main sandbank.

External intervention

By now, the fear of an Iranian victory, with its attendant explosion of religious militancy across the Middle East and the Islamic world, had rallied widespread international support behind Iraq, with the most unlikely bedfellows doing their utmost to ensure that Iraq did not lose this war.

The Soviet Union, Iraq's staunch though problematic ally, which had responded to the invasion of Iran by declaring its neutrality and imposing an arms embargo on Baghdad, resumed arms shipments in mid-1981 once the pendulum had swung in Iran's favor. By the end of the year, considerable quantities of Soviet arms had arrived in Iraq including some 200 T-55 and T-72 tanks and SA-6 surface-to-air missiles. A year later, following the initiation of large-scale Iranian incursions into Iraq, the flow of Soviet arms turned into a flood, and Moscow also extended an offer of (albeit modest) economic support to Baghdad. In return, Saddam declared a general amnesty for the communists and released many of them from jail.

In January 1983 the Soviet Union and Iraq signed an arms deal worth $2 billion, which provided for the supply of T-62 and T-72 tanks, MiG-23 and MiG-25 fighters and Scud B and SS-21 surface-to-surface missiles. By 1987 the Soviet Union had supplied Iraq with large quantities of advanced weaponry, including 800 T-72 tanks and scores of jet fighters and bombers, notably the ultra-modern MiG-29s fitted with the latest radar systems.

The main beneficiary from the temporary setback in Soviet–Iraqi relations had been France. While speaking softly to the Iranians, the French unequivocally nailed their colors to the Iraqi mast from the beginning of the war, taking great pains to accommodate Baghdad's growing need for commercial credits and military hardware: during the first two years of the war France provided Iraq with $5.6 billion worth of weapons, including fighter aircraft, helicopters, tanks,

self-propelled guns, missiles and electronic equipment. This generosity was not difficult to understand. With the Iraqi debt to France more than doubling, from 15 billion francs in 1981 to $5 billion in 1986, the survival of Saddam's personal rule was not only a matter of containing fundamentalist Islam but had also become a prime economic interest.

Egypt, too, was happy to supply Iraq with spare parts and ammunition for its Soviet weapons systems, providing also some 250 T-55 tanks and Tu-16 and Il-28 bombers. These arms were supplemented by light and heavy military vehicles from Spain, armored personnel carriers from Brazil, naval supplies from Italy, and parts for British tanks (captured from the Iranians) from Britain.

Even the United States, whose diplomatic relations with Iraq had been severed by the latter following the 1967 Six Day War, did not shy away from supporting the Iraqi war effort. In February 1982 Baghdad was

Iraqi and Iranian air and missile attacks on each other's population centers, known as the "wars of the cities," had a devastating impact on national morale in the two countries. (Eslami Rad/Gamma)

removed from the US Government's list of states "supporting international terrorism," thus paving the way for a significant boost in US–Iraqi trade relations. Three months later, as the mullahs in Tehran were deliberating the invasion of Iraq, Secretary of State Alexander Haig strongly warned Iran against expanding the war.

In December 1984, merely a month after the re-establishment of diplomatic relations, the newly opened US Embassy in Baghdad began supplying the Iraqi armed forces with much-needed military intelligence. At the same time, Washington nearly doubled its credits for food products and agricultural equipment from $345 million in 1984 to $675 million in 1985; in late 1987 Iraq was promised $1 billion credit for the fiscal year 1988, the largest such credit given to any single country in the world.

In stark contrast to Iraq, Iran found itself with dire logistical problems. The complete suspension of US military support following the revolution (which included the withdrawal of all American advisers and technicians from Iran and the disruption of training programs in the United States) left Iran without a major source of modern weapons and dealt a heavy blow to the logistical capabilities of the armed forces. Thus, for example, the data on the computer-based inventory control system for spares were erased by the US advisers when they left Iran, making it almost impossible for the Iranian military later to locate and identify the mass of spares in depots.

In the initial stages of the war Iran could rely on the substantial inventories of weapons and ordnance built up by the Shah (more indeed, than could be manned or maintained). As the war went on, these stockpiles were impoverished through the cannibalization of unserviceable equipment. This was a direct result of the failure to obtain adequate spares or substitutes.

Fortunately for Iran, it managed to establish a diverse network of arms suppliers, eager to see the prolongation of the war, or at least to derive the utmost benefit from it. Foremost among these were Libya, Syria and North Korea, which together delivered at least 500 tanks (T-55 and T-62), artillery pieces, anti-aircraft weapons and anti-tank missiles. Britain sent spare parts for Chieftain tanks and other armored vehicles by air in 1985. China, Taiwan, Argentina, South Africa, Pakistan and Switzerland also contributed arms, munitions or spares. Even Israel,

Operation Khaibar (February—March 1984) failed to breach the Iraqi defenses near Basra, but managed to capture Majnun Island. Here Iranian naval fighters cross the Iraqi marshland. (Gamma)

second only to the United States in Khomeini's most hated nations, supplied critical items such as F-4 tyres and spare parts for Iran's M-48 and M-60 tanks.

These arms supplies, nevertheless, were far from sufficient. Diversification of weapons presents complications even for advanced, modern armies operating in peacetime conditions. Iran paid a very high price only to realize that a wartime diversification process carried out without a primary source of supply and external advisory and technical support can be a futile experience. Hence, while Iran barely succeeded in maintaining

its major weapons system holdings, Iraq managed to increase and improve its order of battle. Moreover, while the absorption of large quantities of arms enabled Iraq to substantially expand its ground forces, the doubling of Iran's order of battle (from six to 12 divisions) was merely cosmetic. The Iraqi build-up reflected a real growth in operational capabilities, while the Iranian growth stemmed first and foremost from a restructuring of its combat formations, increasing the number of infantry divisions at the expense of the armored divisions, which were in fact disbanded.

Iran's Dawn Offensives 1983–1986

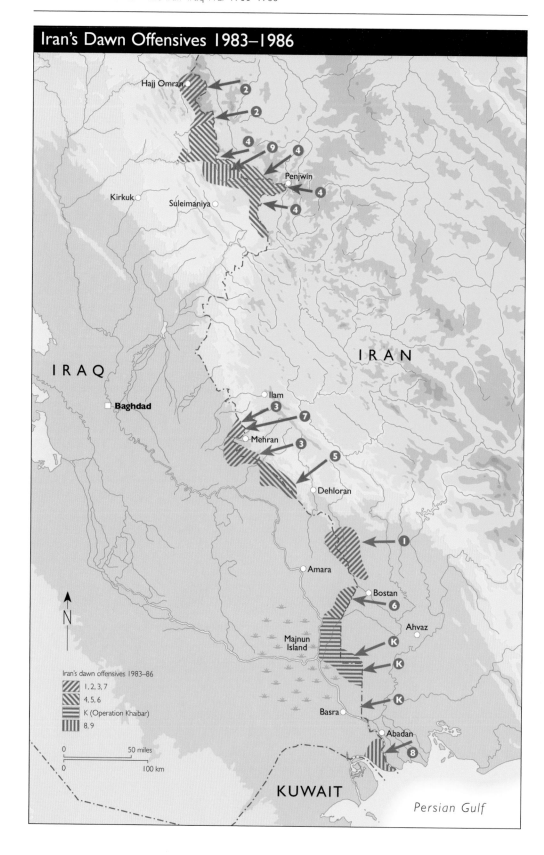

While the shortage of major weapons systems clearly went a long way to determine the direction of this restructuring, political considerations also played an important role. Eager to enhance the status of the Pasdaran and to relegate the army to a subordinate role, the Islamic regime gave clear preference to the creation of new Pasdaran units over the building or reconstruction of regular formations. By 1985, the Pasdaran had been organized in ten divisions, though these had no fixed size or conventional military structure. They were essentially infantry units armed with an unbalanced mix of armaments including tanks, artillery and air defense weapons, but lacking professional sub-units to operate these systems in an orderly way.

The predominance of the Pasdaran, and the transformation of the Iranian army virtually into an infantry force, had a decisive impact on the course of the war. Iran not only failed to attain the overall 3 to 1 superiority normally considered the minimum for a major breakthrough, but also failed to achieve local superiority, owing to Iraq's better mobility. Against this background it was hardly surprising that Iran's ill-equipped infantry, lacking adequate armor, artillery and air support, failed for years to do more than dent the Iraqi defense system.

Stalemate again

Iraq's increased confidence, a result of its growing international support and material superiority, led it to seize the initiative and, on January 28, 1985, to mount its first major offensive since 1980. However, this neither deterred nor frustrated Tehran's preparations for another large offensive of its own. That, duly launched on March 11, 1985, in the direction of Basra, reflected an important shift in Iran's strategy in that it abandoned frontal human-wave assaults in favor of more conventional warfare, carried out under the leadership of the army.

The decision to revert to conventional warfare was apparently taken after the failure of the February 1984 offensive and underscored the revolutionary regime's awareness of both the futility of human-wave tactics and the growing war-weariness in Iran. During 1984 Iran made considerable efforts to transform the Pasdaran into more conventional units and to re-establish a working relationship between it and the army. These efforts bore substantial fruit in the March 1985 offensive, code-named Operation Badr. Inflicting heavy casualties on the Iraqis (reportedly between 10,000 and 12,000, compared with Iran's loss of some 15,000), Iran managed briefly to capture part of the Baghdad–Basra highway nearest the border, thus raising the spectre of cutting Iraq into two. Saddam was shaken and responded by ordering the widest use of chemical weapons to date (by this time the Iraqis had already extended their use of chemical agents beyond mustard gas to include such agents as tabun and cyanide) as well as a massive air and missile campaign against some 30 Iranian towns and cities including Tehran, Tabriz, Isfahan and Bushehr. Iran immediately responded in kind, and within a fortnight the second war of the cities had been fought.

As the ground war settled into immobility the focus of operations shifted back to the strategic sphere, with both states attacking civilian shipping and strategic targets, such as population centers and industrial complexes. In mid-August 1985, frustration at Iran's stubborn prosecution of the war led Iraq to play what many considered to be its trump card: between August 15 and late December, nearly 60 air raids against the main Iranian oil complex at Kharg Island were recorded. This intense campaign met with only limited success, but it seems to have worried Iran. Recognizing perhaps that attacks on Kharg, to which it had no effective response, could do more damage to its war effort than any major offensive, Iran tried to deter Iraq by intensifying air raids on Iraqi towns and cities, waylaying ships passing through the Strait of Hormuz to check whether or not they were carrying war goods bound for Iraq, declaring a partial mobilization, and, above all, preparing for yet another big offensive.

The Fao turning point

When it eventually came on February 9, 1986, Operation Dawn 8 turned out to be Iran's greatest success since the expulsion of Iraqi forces from its territory. Iran managed to breach the Iraqi line at several points, to capture the Fao Peninsula at the south-eastern tip of Iraq, and to retain it despite repeated Iraqi attempts to dislodge the attackers.

Planned by the army's general staff, the Iranian offensive consisted of a two-pronged attack, involving some 100,000 troops (five regular divisions and approximately 50,000 Pasdaran and Basij fighters). The northern effort—apparently a diversionary attack—was directed against Basra and was easily repulsed. Yet Iraq's preoccupation with the defense of Basra was skilfully exploited by Iran to achieve a large measure of tactical surprise and to capture Fao in less than 24 hours of fighting. The Iraqis were further constrained by an extraordinary all-night torrential rain storm that prevented them from bringing into effect their overwhelming air and artillery superiority in order to intercept the Iranian men, vehicles, weapons and equipment being ferried across the Shatt al-Arab.

Once they realized the extent of the Iranian success, the Iraqis mounted a three-pronged counterattack on February 12, only to be contained by the Iranians after a week of heavy fighting. Saddam peremptorily ordered Maher Abd al-Rashid, his kinsman and one of Iraq's best performing military commanders during the war, to take personal command of the offensive. Bringing with him fresh formations of Republican Guards, Iraq's elite force, and assisted by some of Iraq's foremost officers, notably generals Hisham Fakhri

(Commander of the Seventh Army Corps) and Saad Tuma Abbas, al-Rashid resumed the offensive on February 24. Yet, despite their overwhelming superiority in firepower and their resort to chemical weapons, the Iraqi forces failed to retake Fao, with some 10,000 Iraqis (and 30,000 Iranians) killed in a fortnight.

Four years later, during his famous meeting with the US Ambassador to Baghdad, April Glaspie, and shortly before Iraq's invasion of Kuwait, Saddam would turn this humiliating defeat into a shining achievement. "Yours is a nation that cannot afford to lose 10,000 men in one battle," he boasted in front of the startled ambassador. Yet in February–March 1986 Saddam's situation looked very bleak indeed. Having rebuffed the Iraqi counterattack, Iranian forces broke out of Fao and made their way towards Umm Qasr. Had this follow-up attack succeeded, Iran would have severed Iraq from the Gulf and would have become Kuwait's immediate neighbor. As things were, the Iranian offensive was checked. Yet the fall of Fao sent shock-waves all over the Gulf and the Arab world, with the Saudi and Kuwaiti foreign ministers pleading with Syria, Iran's closest Arab ally, to use its good offices in Tehran. The anxiety of the Gulf states was further exacerbated by the launching of a large Iranian offensive in Kurdistan, which managed to capture some ground and to advance within a few miles of Suleimaniya.

Though this northern offensive was eventually bogged down, Iraq's inability to dislodge Iran from Fao was an important psychological victory for Iran and a heavy blow to Saddam's prestige and the morale of the Iraqi armed forces. After four years of persistent thrusts into Iraq, Iran managed to gain a significant foothold on Iraqi territory, and the revolutionary regime was determined to exploit this success to the full both for propaganda and for morale-boosting purposes.

In these circumstances, Saddam was understandably desperate for some visible successes. In mid-May 1986, in a massively

ABOVE and RIGHT The capture of the Fao Peninsula in February 1986 marked the high point of Iran's repeated incursions into Iraq. (Gamma)

publicized operation, Iraq took the Iranian town of Mehran on the central front (again with the use of gas) and offered to exchange it for Fao. The offer was spurned and Iranian forces recaptured Mehran in early July. This success seems to have increased Tehran's confidence, with Iranian leaders reiterating their determination to deal a "final blow" to the Iraqi regime.

Anxious to fend off yet another large-scale offensive, on August 3, 1986, Saddam made a desperate plea for peace in the form of an "open letter" to the Iranian leadership. Gone were his earlier pretensions to Gulf, let alone Arab, leadership. Apart from a vague reference to future Iraqi–Iranian collaboration over the stability of the Gulf, Saddam's conditions for peace centered on the security of his regime, namely, a guarantee to respect each other's choice of government. When Tehran remained as adamant as ever on his removal from power,

Saddam concluded that his only hope of persuading the Iranian authorities to desist from their efforts to overthrow him was to appeal to them indirectly by making life still more unpleasant for their constituents. Accordingly, an unprecedentedly ferocious aerial campaign was launched against Iranian strategic targets, primarily the Kharg Island oil complex, and major population centers—including Tehran, Isfahan, and Kermanshah. On August 12, 1986, Iraqi aircraft mounted the first successful raid on the Iranian oil terminal of Sirri Island (some 150 miles [240 km] north of the Strait of Hormuz), thereby signaling to Tehran that no strategic targets were beyond Iraq's operational reach.

The tanker war

Iraq also intensified its attacks on civilian shipping, particularly tankers, moving to and from Iran. The so-called "tanker war" was launched by Saddam in early 1984 with a view to shifting the war from the stalemate of the battlefield to a new and potentially more rewarding arena. Both parties had, of course, carried out attacks against each other's merchant shipping since the early stages of the war; between September 1980 and February 1984, 23 Iraqi and 5 Iranian attacks were recorded. In 1984 alone, however, there were 37 Iraqi and 17 Iranian attacks.

The tanker war differed from the previous campaign against shipping not only in its scope but also in its strategic rationale. Unlike earlier Iraqi attacks on civilian shipping, which were directed solely against Iran and were aimed at convincing it of the futility of continuing the war, the tanker war sought to draw other states—the western powers in particular—into the war, in the hope that they would support Iraq or help to bring about a peaceful settlement. The idea seems to have been that intensifying the attacks would provoke Iran into extreme actions, such as attempts to close the Strait of Hormuz, at the southern tip of the Gulf, which would leave the Western oil consumers (the United States in particular) with no alternative but to intervene.

These expectations were ostensibly based on solid grounds. The mullahs had repeatedly warned that "if Iran's oil shipping were halted, then no country in the world will be able to use the Persian Gulf oil." The Western response to the Iranian threats also

seemed to vindicate the Iraqi assumptions. The United States, for instance, warned Iran off such a course of action and announced its determination to keep the Gulf open to international shipping. It even took care to demonstrate its resolve by sending a task force (of three warships with some 2,000 marines) to the Indian Ocean on October 13, 1983.

It was against this backdrop that Iraq warned in late November 1983 that all merchant vessels should avoid the "war zone" at the northern end of the Gulf, and, on January 29, 1984, broadened this threat to include all shipping around Kharg Island, Iran's main oil refinery. Beginning in February 1984, Iraqi attacks on tankers sailing to or from Kharg increased until they reached an average of four a month.

Iran's response to these moves to escalate the war did not live up to Saddam's expectations. Fully aware of the rationale

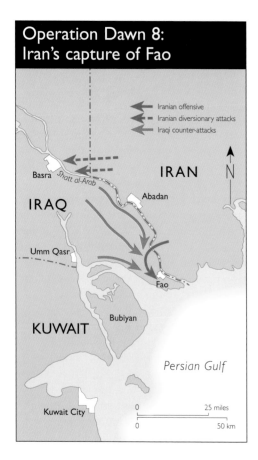

Operation Dawn 8: Iran's capture of Fao

Iranian offensive
Iranian diversionary attacks
Iraqi counter-attacks

IRAN

Basra
Shatt al-Arab

Abadan

IRAQ

Umm Qasr

Fao

KUWAIT

Bubiyan

Persian Gulf

Kuwait City

0   25 miles

0   50 km

N

behind the Iraqi strategy, Iran not only avoided any attempt to block the Strait of Hormuz, but went out of its way to keep its responses at the lowest possible level; it refrained from public acknowledgement of its attacks on civilian shipping, and reiterated its disinclination to close the Strait since "the Islamic Republic of Iran would be the first to suffer as a result of such a move." Iranian naval attacks were essentially limited to ships trading with Saudi Arabia and Kuwait, in the hope that these two countries, Iraq's staunch economic supporters, would exert economic pressure on Iraq to end its attacks. When Saudi Arabian F-15s shot down an Iranian jet on June 5, the Iranian protest was extremely muted.

To Saddam's dismay, Iran's caution succeeded in keeping the Western powers relatively aloof. Although the eruption of the tanker war increased American anxiety and reportedly led to a review of Gulf contingency plans, it was not followed by any concrete action. It was only in late 1986, after the intensification of the Iraqi campaign against Iranian economic targets and commercial shipping, that Iranian caution began to falter. Responding to the Iraqi escalation by intensifying its own attacks on Iraq-bound shipping, Tehran intimidated Kuwait to the point that it approached both superpowers, requesting protection for a number of its tankers against naval attacks. In March 1987 the United States informed the Kuwaiti government of its willingness to escort Kuwait's 11 tankers through the Gulf, provided they would fly the US flag, and a month later Kuwait chartered three tankers from the USSR, which were put under the Soviet flag. By the end of 1987 Iran was confronted with a formidable multinational armada of nearly 50 warships.

The turning of the tide

Shielded by the West from Tehran's wrath, Iraq could intensify its attacks on Iran-bound shipping and oil infrastructure with virtual impunity. It did exactly that in the hope that the Iranians would sooner or later provide the West with a pretext to unleash its power on them. Although this assessment proved misconceived, as Tehran did its best to signal its interest in de-escalation, the Iraqi pressure further damaged the Iranian economy, while the multinational presence in the Gulf exacerbated the feeling of isolation and hopelessness within the Iranian leadership.

Meanwhile Iran was finding it impossible to make any headway on the battlefield, as relations between the Pasdaran and the army deteriorated yet again. As the regime's praetorian guard, with political, religious and civil tasks on top of its military ones, by 1986 the Pasdaran had become a substantial force of some 350,000 troops, equal in size to the army but enjoying preferential treatment from the authorities. This included numerous privileges, such as superior pay and benefits to those enjoyed by the military, better access to the political leadership, and first call on arms, spare parts, and recruits. In September 1985, preparations for the establishment of Pasdaran air and naval forces began in earnest following a special directive from Khomeini, and the following year the Pasdaran started an "advanced artillery training" and designated a special corps for this. Needless to say, the professional army was less than thrilled by these persistent encroachments on operational fields that had hitherto been its exclusive preserve.

Increasingly frustrated by the renewed stalemate, in April 1986 Khomeini issued a religious ruling (*fatwa*) instructing his forces to win the war by March 21, 1987, the Iranian New Year. In compliance with their spiritual leader's wish, on December 24, 1986, a major offensive was launched in the direction of Basra. Planned and executed by Hashemi-Rafsanjani himself, against the wishes of the military leaders, Operation Karbala 4 sought to overwhelm the defending Iraqi forces in a night attack by sheer weight of numbers. This was not to happen. Bringing to full effect their superior firepower, the Iraqis held their ground,

killing some 10,000 Iranians in three days of ferocious fighting. Yet this bloody failure did not dampen Iranian enthusiasm, and in January 1987 another attack was launched in the same sector of the front. Code-named Operation Karbala 5, the new offensive managed to cross the Shatt al-Arab and to seize some territory, at the cost of several thousand casualties, but once again failed to breach the Iraqi line of defense.

By now, however, Iraqi combat performance had significantly improved.

Following the humiliating string of military setbacks in 1986, Saddam was confronted, for the first and only time in his career, by what nearly amounted to an open mutiny. With the Iranian army at the gates of Basra, the military leadership rose up in an attempt to force Saddam to win the war despite himself. Fortunately for the Iraqi president, the generals did not demand political power or try to overthrow him. All they wanted was the professional freedom to run the war according to their best judgement, with

In an attempt to curtail Iran's oil exports and to draw international intervention in the war, in 1984 Saddam Hussein launched sustained attacks against Iranian and Iranian-bound shipping. With Iran responding in kind the two sides found themselves locked for years in what came to be known as the "tanker war." (Gamma)

minimal interference from the political authorities.

Perhaps the most vivid illustration of this "rebellious" state of mind is offered by the oft-repeated story about Saddam's clash in the winter of 1986 with Maher Abd al-Rashid. According to the story, Rashid was ordered to report back to Baghdad following his failure to dislodge the Iranian forces from the Fao Peninsula, and his candid admission in an interview with the Kuwaiti press of high casualties on the Iraqi side. Well aware of what the order meant, Rashid's officers transmitted a warning to Saddam, implying that they would refuse to prosecute the war should anything happen to their commander. On arriving at the Presidential Palace, Rashid was decorated by a beaming Saddam, who deferred vengeance until later.

The officers' exceptional determination to stand up to Saddam saved Iraq from disaster. Caught between the hammer and the anvil, Saddam gave in to his generals and the war gradually took a positive turn. In early 1987 the army rebuffed Iran's last large offensive during the war, and the next year it moved on to the offensive.

In all these operations Iraq made extensive use of chemical weapons, which, apart from Saddam's determination to get the Iranians off Iraqi territory at all costs, reflected the generals' lax attitude towards this operational mode. For all his lack of moral inhibitions and respect for international norms, Saddam's overwhelming preoccupation with his political survival injected a strong element of restraint into his behavior, which his generals lacked completely. For them chemical weapons were yet another category of armament whose use depended purely on their military value in the relevant circumstances. As Abd al-Rashid put it, "If you gave me a pesticide to throw at these swarms of insects to make them breathe and become exterminated, I would use it."

No one knew this better than the Iraqi Kurds. In 1987 and 1988 they were subjected to a brutal punitive campaign involving the extensive use of chemical weapons, including mustard gas, cyanide, and tabun nerve agent against an unprotected civilian population. The first attacks of this kind were reported in May 1987, when some

The tanker war

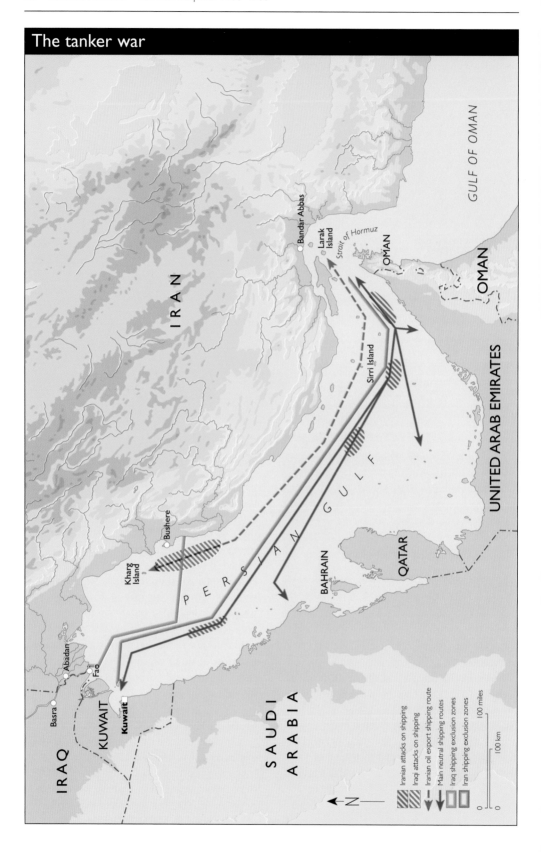

Iranian attacks on shipping

Iraqi attacks on shipping

Iranian oil export shipping route

Main neutral shipping routes

Iraq shipping exclusion zones

Iran shipping exclusion zones

Following the intensification of the tanker war, the United States agreed to protect Kuwaiti tankers in the Gulf. (Gamma)

20 Kurdish villages were gassed in an attempt to deter the civilian population from collaborating with the advancing Iranian forces. A month later several Kurdish villages in Iran were given the same "medicine," killing some 100 people and injuring 2,000. The most appalling attack took place in March 1988, when the spectre of an Iranian breakthrough drove the Iraqi forces to employ gas on an unprecedented scale against the Kurdish town of Halabja. As the thick cloud of gas spread by the Iraqi planes on March 16 evaporated into the clear sky, television crews were rushed into the town by the Iranians and the world saw the full extent of the massacre. Five thousand people—men, women, children and babies—were killed that day. Nearly 10,000 suffered injuries.

The Iranians were little better equipped than the Kurds to deal with Iraq's chemical attacks. Their chemical arsenals were a far cry from those of Iraq, their stocks of protective gear were meager, and many of them would not even take the elementary precaution of shaving their beards before wearing gas masks. Their strongest weapon against Iraqi chemical warfare was essentially political—namely, the propaganda value derived from the Iraqi attacks. Yet, even in this respect they did not fare too well. At that time Saddam was the favorite son of the West (and to a lesser extent the Soviet Union), the perceived barrier to the spread of Islamic fundamentalism. Consequently, apart from occasional feeble remonstrations (notably after the Halabja attack), Western governments were consciously willing to turn a blind eye to Iraq's chemical excesses.

This aloofness was further reinforced by the fact that by the spring of 1988, for the first time in eight years, the end of the war was in prospect and the Western powers (as well as the Soviet Union) were not going to do anything that could delay such an eventuality. The Iranian campaign seemed to be running out of steam. The sense of purpose among Iranians had gradually declined after mid-1982, when they were no longer defending their own territory but were engaged on Iraqi soil. Economic dislocations occasioned by fighting gave rise

to great frustration as shortages of basic commodities grew worse, and a black market and corruption flourished. A mounting human toll caused a deep war-weariness.

Seeing the light at the end of the tunnel for the first time since the early months of the war, in late February 1988 Saddam ordered the fifth, and most ferocious, war of the cities. During the next two months over

LEFT and BELOW Iran's last attempt to capture Basra in January—February 1987 (code-named Karbala 5) was repelled with great effort and through the use of chemical weapons. (Gamma)

200 surface-to-surface missiles and numerous air raids battered Iran's major population centers. The risks of this escalation for Iraq were negligible. Iran was in no position to launch a ground offensive due to the lack of volunteers for the front, nor was it capable of extending the war to Iraq's hinterland, given its glaring strategic inferiority. All Tehran could do was intensify attacks against Iraq-bound shipping; but such a move involved the risk of a direct confrontation with the United States, which Iran was anxious to avoid.

The fifth war of the cities thus turned out to be the straw that broke Iranian morale. With government employees joining other citizens in fleeing Tehran *en masse*, the regime was paralyzed and national morale was shattered to the core. The road from there to the total collapse of the military's fighting spirit was short. In mid-April 1988, after nearly six years in a defensive posture, Iraq moved to the offensive, and in 48 hours of fierce fighting recaptured the Fao Peninsula, the loss of which in 1986 had marked Baghdad's lowest ebb during the war. A major psychological victory for Iraq, the recapture of Fao signaled the final shift in fortunes during the war. It was soon followed by a string of military successes: at the end of May Iraq drove the Iranians out of their positions in Salamcheh (east of Basra), and the following month dislodged them from Majnun Island, held by Iran since 1985. On July 13, Iraq threatened that it would invade southern Iran unless Iran immediately withdrew its remaining forces from Kurdistan. And while Iran publicly complied with this demand on the following day, Iraq nevertheless captured a small strip of Iranian territory in the central part of the front, for the first time since 1982, then withdrew behind its frontier.

These setbacks were compounded by Iran's growing difficulties in the Gulf, primarily the intensification of the American (and other Western) naval presence there. For most of the war's duration, direct American involvement in the conflict had been surprisingly meager; it manifested itself

Operation Karbala 5 (January—February 1987)

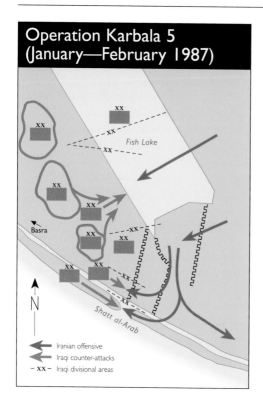

Fish Lake

Basra

Shatt al-Arab

N

◄── Iranian offensive
◄── Iraqi counter-attacks
─ xx ─ Iraqi divisional areas

Some 5,000 people were killed and nearly 10,000 suffered injuries when Iraqi airplanes gassed the Iraqi Kurdish town of Halabja in March 1988. (Gamma)

in diplomatic and limited military support for the Gulf Arab states and Iraq. From 1984 onwards the US sought to compel Iran to accept a ceasefire by severing it from any weapons sources (Operation Staunch), but in 1985–1986 Washington deviated from its own strategy and secretly sold arms to Iran in return for the release of US hostages held in Lebanon. The embarrassing exposure of this affair (quickly dubbed Irangate) drove the US to more vigorous efforts to contain the war. While the most visible manifestation of this change of tack was undoubtedly the US Administration's agreement to reflag (and protect) 11 Kuwaiti tankers, Washington's efforts to terminate the war had a diplomatic component as well, namely the engineering of Security Council Resolution 598 of July 1987 calling for an end to the conflict, and the orchestration of the so-called "second resolution," which called for a UN-enforced arms embargo on Iran for its failure to abide by Resolution 598.

The American arrival in the Gulf in the summer of 1987 was viewed by Iran with the utmost alarm. It presented Tehran with an omnipotent foe and threatened to tie its

An Iraqi soldier celebrates the recapture of the Fao Peninsula in front of a bullet-ridden portrait of Khomeini. (Gamma)

hands in the ongoing tanker war, while leaving Iraq free to attack Iran-bound shipping. Hence, notwithstanding a measure of muscle-flexing, Iran sought to avoid a direct confrontation with the United States and to signal its interest in de-escalation. And indeed, with the exception of a brief American–Iranian exchange in September–October 1987, a direct collision between the two countries was avoided until April 18, 1988. This clash, following the holing of a US frigate by an underwater mine, could not have come at a more inopportune time for Iran as it coincided with the dislodging of Iranian forces from Fao. The result was an Iranian attempt at retaliation, and the subsequent loss of a significant portion of Iran's naval force: six vessels including two (out of three) frigates.

The ground was thus set for a radical change of policy. At the beginning of June, Iran's parliamentary Speaker, Hashemi-Rafsanjani, was appointed acting Commander-in-Chief of the armed forces, while Mohsen Rezai, the commander of the Pasdaran, was forced publicly to own up for the recent military defeats. These moves were widely seen within Iran as a prelude to

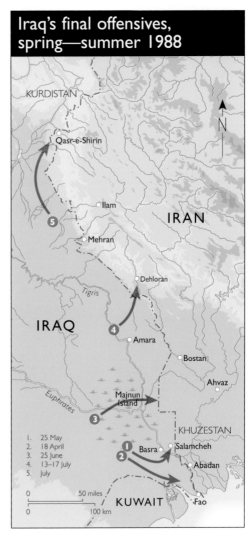

Iraq's final offensives, spring—summer 1988

KURDISTAN

Qasr-e-Shirin

Ilam

IRAN

Mehran

Dehloran

Tigris

IRAQ

Amara

Bostan

Ahvaz

Majnun Island

Euphrates

KHUZESTAN

1. 25 May
2. 18 April
3. 25 June
4. 13–17 July
5. July

Basra

Salamcheh

Abadan

0   50 miles

0   100 km

KUWAIT

Fao

Ali Akbar Hashemi-Rafsanjani, the powerful Speaker of the Iranian Parliament and a relentless hawk for most of the war, was instrumental in convincing Khomeini to cease fire. (Gamma)

the war's termination, and, indeed, were followed by desperate attempts by the clerics to convince Khomeini to sanctify the cessation of hostilities. Iraq was not the only enemy facing Iran, they reasoned in an attempt to convince the aged ayatollah to accept the unthinkable. Rather, a worldwide coalition of imperialist forces, headed by the Great Satan (the United States), vied for Iranian blood. Therefore, and in view of the social and economic conditions in Iran, any prolongation of the war could but play into the aggressors' hands and would endanger the great achievements of the Islamic Revolution. What could provide a better proof of imperialist ruthlessness, they retorted, than the shooting down (on July 3) of an Iranian civilian plane by the US navy and the killing of its 290 passengers?

Paradoxically, the airline tragedy turned out to be the means for an Iranian climbdown. It provided the moral cover of martyrdom and suffering in the face of an unjust superior force that allowed the regime to camouflage the comprehensive defeat of its international vision. In mid-July a meeting of the Iranian leadership took place, presided over by Ahmed Khomeini, the ayatollah's eldest son, who deputized for his ailing father. Reportedly marked by much recrimination, the meeting's final recommendation was an immediate ceasefire. On July 17, 1988, after a year of evasion and procrastination, President Khameini sent a letter to the UN Secretary-General, Javier Perez de Cuellar, expressing his country's acceptance of a ceasefire. "We have decided to declare officially," read the letter, "that the Islamic Republic of Iran—because of the importance it attaches to saving the lives of human beings and the establishment of justice and regional and international peace and security—accepts UN Resolution 598."

Iran's boy soldiers

Of the many battlefield spectacles of the Iran-Iraq War, none has struck and confounded foreign observers more than the blind devotion of the Basij and their relentless quest for martyrdom. Coming mainly from rural areas or from the most devout Shi'ite families, these poorly trained and ill-equipped youths, some as young as 12, were little more than canon fodder or human minesweepers sent in advance of Iran's other military forces to clear the fields, desert scrubland and marshes. With their red and yellow headbands proclaiming Allah's or Khomeini's greatness, a piece of white cloth pinned to their uniforms as symbol of a shroud, each one carrying his death with him, and a plastic key around their necks, issued personally by Khomeini as a symbol of their assured entry into paradise upon martyrdom, they charged towards the Iraqi positions in total disregard of the danger

to their lives, and to the shocked disbelief of their enemies. "They come on in their hundreds, often walking straight across the minefields, triggering them with their feet as they are supposed to do," an Iraqi officer described the effect of these assaults on him and his men:

They chant "Allahu Akbar" and they keep coming, and we keep shooting, sweeping our 50 millimeter machine guns around like sickles. My men are eighteen, nineteen, just a few years older than these kids. I've seen them crying, and at times the officers have had to kick them back to their guns. Once we had Iranian kids on bikes cycling towards us, and my men all started laughing, and then these kids started lobbing their hand grenades and we stopped laughing and started shooting.

What was the source of this unqualified readiness for self-sacrifice? Were these child-warriors brainwashed by the authorities? Were they coerced? Not

according to Ahmed, who was 14 when he volunteered to defend his homeland against the Iraqi invasion. "When Khorramshahr was recaptured by our troops in 1982, I made up my mind to go to the front," he told a Western humanitarian aid worker who spent some time trying to help captured Basij boys in Iraqi prisoner camps. "I wanted to defend my country, that's all."

BELOW and LEFT Iran's fearless teenage soldiers. Some even lied about their age to be accepted in the army. Their headlong attacks forced Iraqi soldiers to fire in self-defense, despite being aware that the attackers were only children. (Rex Features/Gamma)

What about the concept of martyrdom? Did he join the forces with the explicit desire to martyr himself?

I am not very religious so I don't know much about the subject. It's true that martyrdom is important to Shi'ites—we all learn about the Imams and how they died—but I didn't go to war to die for Islam. I went to defend Iran and I think most of my friends went for the same reason.

Was Ahmed, or anyone he knew, forced in any way to join up? The answer was an unequivocal no:

In my case, my father and mother never wanted me to go to the front. Neither did my teacher. But I was determined to go. I've never heard any stories of mothers forcing their sons to join the basij. It was the opposite case with all my friends and I can't believe that a mother went on television to say that about her own child. My mother loves me and writes to me here to say how much she misses me and that she wants to see me again.

I was so determined to go to war that I ran away from home. The first time I was sent back home because the officer said I was too young—I was thirteen at the time. The second time I tried was a year later when I was fourteen. I went to the local HQ of the basij. The officer told me that I had to be fifteen to join up, so I told him I was. He wanted to see my identity card, so I gave it to him, and he saw I was only fourteen. Then he asked what my parents had said, because he needed their permission if I joined before I was fifteen. I said they agreed and he allowed me to join up. There were hundreds of young boys pushing to get into the office that morning. All were very young, so the officer had no choice but to let us in.

Did he consider himself a victim of the regime? An innocent bystander lured into the whirlpool of war by the sheer weight of propaganda? Absolutely not, protested Ahmed:

Of course there was a campaign to recruit men into the army. Our country was threatened by invasion. It's normal to want to defend it. So mullahs would come to the schools to talk to us and we watched military programs on the television which told us what was going on in the war. But no one influenced my decision. At fourteen I could decide things for myself and I wanted to go to war, so I went. It was as simple as that.

Not all Basij fighters had such unquestioning patriotic zeal. Ahmed's fellow prisoner of war, Samir, had a far more disillusioned view of the Basij phenomenon and its motivation. "It was a game for us," he said:

On the television they would show a young boy dressed as a soldier, carrying a gun and wearing the red headband of the basij. He would say how wonderful it was to be a soldier for Islam, fighting for freedom against the Iraqis. Then he would curse the Iraqis and all Arabs, saying they were not good Muslims. Next he would tell us to join him and come to war. We didn't understand the words "patriotism" or "martyrdom," or at least I didn't. It was just an exciting game and a chance to prove to your friends that you'd grown up and were no longer a child. But we were really only children.

At school there were always mullahs coming to speak to us and interrupting our lessons. The teacher didn't like them coming, but he was too afraid to say anything in case he lost his job. They talked about the glorious Islamic Revolution and the Ayatollah who had rescued us from the hands of the Americans. Then we would chant, "death to America, death to Israel, death to Saddam" for a long time. The mullahs said it was an honor to go and fight for Islam and to be martyred for Islam, just like Imam Hussein [son of Ali, the Shia's patron imam]. I didn't want to die for anyone, but wanted to stay at school. My mother and father wanted me to stay at school, too. When I left for the war, my mother was crying. My father didn't say anything, but I could see he was very sad. My mother begged me not to go, holding and kissing me on the head, screaming for me not to go. My father had to pull her away to let me leave the house. I should have stayed, but all my friends were leaving, too, and I was excited about going. I had already done some training in the camp and I knew how to use a gun and throw hand grenades.

What did he think of the impact of the regime's wider propaganda effort, such as the screening of mass demonstrations by Basij warriors on television? Though not giving a definite answer, Samir's own experience would seem to vindicate the powerful pull of "mob mentality" on the undecided individual:

I took part in those demonstrations. They gave us red headbands to wear and we all stood in the square in the middle of Tehran . . . Twice there were TV cameras to film us. The mullahs were at the front, directing us. We would shout various slogans against Israel, America, France and, of course, Saddam, the President of Iraq. He was worse than the rest put together. After the slogans, the mullahs would address the crowds, telling us what an honor it was for us to be going to fight and die for Islam. I have no idea why I was shouting, since I

don't have any bad feelings against America. Many Iranians live in America and Europe, so it can't be all that bad.

Looking back at the whole experience, did Samir deem it worthwhile? And should young boys be recruited for front-line fighting in the first place?

I am not sure, but it was difficult to stop them. And anyway, the boys who attacked the Iraqis were a very important weapon for the army, because they had no fear. We captured many positions from the Iraqis because they became afraid when they saw young boys running towards them shouting and screaming. Imagine how you would feel. Lots of boys were killed, but by that stage you were running and couldn't stop, so you just carried on until you were shot yourself or reached the lines.

I'm glad I was captured, even though it's very hard to live in the prisoner-of-war camps. But anything is better than dying. If I have a son I will never let him go to war until he is old enough to understand and make up his own mind. I was too young to fight. I was a little boy who wanted to play with guns. When they gave me a real one I'd never been happier. But when I went to fight and shoot people, I was petrified.

Nations at war

Ever since war was transformed in the late 18th century from a contest between professional armies into a clash between populations, its prosecution has become decisively linked to the vicissitudes of national morale. No regime can sustain a prolonged war unless a significant portion of the nation endorses the effort and is willing to make sacrifices necessary to its prosecution. History is littered with cases where the stronger belligerent, having misjudged its national morale, has failed to translate a marked military superiority into political gain (e.g. the United States in Vietnam, Israel in Lebanon).

This reality has never been lost on Saddam Hussein. He reckoned that the Iraqi people could be rallied behind a cause of grave national interest. Yet he had no illusions regarding the people's willingness to make heavy sacrifices for the maintenance of his personal rule. The war with Iran arose primarily from the hostility between the Islamic regime in Iran and Iraq's ruling Ba'th party, or, more specifically, the personal animosity between Saddam and Khomeini; in these circumstances, the support of the Iraqi people, especially of the majority Shi'ite community, could not be taken for granted.

The export of the Iranian Revolution did not threaten Iraq as a nation state. Rather, it was Saddam and the Ba'th leadership that were targeted as "public enemies" by the aged ayatollah. Khomeini had no territorial designs on Iraq or enmity towards its people. On the contrary, he repeatedly emphasized that "we do not wish the ordinary people, the innocent people to be hurt." All he wanted was the substitution of a pious leadership for the "infidel" regime in Baghdad.

Shielding Iraqis from the war

By way of persuading his subjects that his decision to make war was theirs, Saddam carried the extensive personality cult, which had already been under way before the war, to an extraordinary peak of propaganda and forced adulation even by the standards of the Middle East's highly personalized politics. The Iraqi people were inescapably exposed to the towering presence of the

By way of rallying the Iraqi people behind the war effort Saddam carried his extensive personality cult to new peaks of propaganda and forced adulation. (Gamma)

"Struggler President," from the moment they glanced at the morning paper, through their journey to work, to the family evening gathering in front of the television or the radio. They saw him posing with a rocket launcher on the front lines or paternally embracing young children; as a statesman meeting heads of state and as a military leader discussing war plans; as an efficient bureaucrat in a trendy suit and as an ordinary peasant, helping farmers with their harvest, scythe in hand. His portraits pervaded the country to such an extent that a popular joke put Iraq's population at 26 million: 13 million Iraqis and 13 million pictures of Saddam.

This personality cult was accompanied by strenuous efforts to insulate the general Iraqi population from the effects of the war. Instead of concentrating most of Iraq's resources on the military effort and, like Iran, stressing the virtue of sacrifice, the Iraqi president sought to prove to his people that he could wage war and maintain a business-as-usual atmosphere at the same time. Ambitious development plans that had commenced prior to the war went ahead, and public spending rose from $21 billion in 1980 to $29.5 billion in 1982. The lion's share of this expanded budget (up from only $13.9 billion in 1980) was spent on civilian imports to prevent commodity shortages.

The outcome of this guns-and-butter policy was that the ferocious war that raged on the battlefield was hardly felt on the Iraqi home front. Instead, the country was buzzing with economic activity, to the delight of numerous foreign contractors, Western in particular, who leisurely carved lucrative slices from the expanding Iraqi economy. Construction projects of all sorts, begun prior to the war, continued apace, and Baghdad was being transformed at a feverish pace from a medieval into a modern city. Daily life in the capital continued largely unaffected. Blackouts, imposed at the beginning of the war, were quickly lifted once the seriously disabled and dwindling Iranian air force was unable to extend the war to the Iraqi hinterland. Most foodstuffs were readily available, and the black color of mourning was not too visible in the streets of Baghdad. The most salient signs of war were the growing number of women in government offices and the swelling numbers of Asian and Arab workers who poured into Baghdad to replace Iraqis who were fulfilling their national duty at the front.

To be sure, the effort to insulate the Iraqi population from the dislocations of the war could not be fully successful. After all, a nation of merely 13 million people can hardly remain impervious to many thousands of casualties (even the authorities were forced to admit to some 1,200 casualties per month). However, to a large extent the protective shield built by Saddam cushioned the Iraqi public from the hazards of war, and those directly involved in the fighting or personally affected by the war were handsomely rewarded by the authorities. The already high standard of living of the officer corps was further improved, and members of the armed forces were given priority for car and house purchases. Bereaved families, for their part, earned a free car, a free plot of land and an interest-free loan to build a house.

While eliminating potential public dissatisfaction with the war through his domestic policy, Saddam paid close attention to the only state organ that could effectively endanger his regime—the military. Forcing his colleagues in the ruling Ba'th Party to follow him in substituting the ubiquitous battledress for their tailored suits, he transformed the Revolutionary Command Council into his personal headquarters, thus maintaining tight control of war operations. This was clearly demonstrated by an apparent inflexibility and lack of initiative on the part of Iraq's field commanders. Battalion and brigade commanders were unwilling to make independent decisions in rapidly changing battlefield situations, instead referring back to division or corps headquarters, which in turn approached the highest command in Baghdad.

Saddam also extended the logic of his inconspicuous war to include the complete subordination of war operations to political considerations. Aware of the complex composition of Iraq's population and reluctant to risk significant losses within any of Iraq's sectarian groups, he instructed the military leadership to prepare and execute the invasion with the utmost caution, so as to minimize casualties. This instruction, which went against the view of Saddam's professional advisers, had devastating consequences. Not only did it fail to reduce casualties, it actually increased them when Iraq, unable to exploit its initial successes, was forced to commit its troops in worsening operational conditions as Iran strengthened its defenses.

Surviving the Iranian assault

By mid-1982, as Iran began its determined drives into Iraq, the butter-and-guns policy,

perhaps the main buttress of Iraqi national morale, had to be abandoned because of the war's drain on the country's financial reserves and loss of oil revenues due to the war with Iran and the world oil glut; this predicament was compounded by Syria's closure of the Iraqi pipeline to Banias on the Mediterranean (Damascus was then Iran's closest Arab ally), which slashed Iraq's expected oil revenues by $5 billion. With Iraqi foreign reserves plunging from $35 billion before the war to $3 billion at the end of 1983, the government had to cut back on much non-essential spending and to adopt austerity measures. Consequently civilian imports dropped from a peak of $21.5 billion in 1982 to $12.2 billion in

As the military situation deteriorated, the Iraqi regime was increasingly forced to resort to mass public campaigns to service the declining Iraqi economy. (Gamma)

1983, and $10–11 billion per annum between 1984 and 1987.

As the situation on the front deteriorated in early 1986, Saddam embarked on a sustained campaign to mobilize Iraqi society to the war effort. All Iraqis were urged to donate money, blood and working hours, and some 100,000 men, women and children were enlisted to cut reeds in the southern marshes, with a view to facilitating military operations there. In an attempt to offset Iran's overwhelming demographic superiority, Saddam personally launched a nationwide campaign to encourage procreation. "Our motto must be that each family produces five children and that families failing to produce at least four children deserve to be harshly reprimanded," he declared, advising female students to choose child-bearing over studies.

Paradoxically, the reversal in Iraq's military fortunes facilitated Saddam's efforts to rally the nation behind him. Once Iraq was no longer operating on foreign soil but rather defending its own homeland, the armed forces regained their fighting spirit and public morale became buoyant. Saddam was seemingly able to avoid the taint of defeat and to portray the war as a heroic defense of the nation, and by extension of the Arab world, against a bigoted and aggressive enemy who persistently sabotaged efforts for peace.

Well before the war Saddam had assiduously been harnessing Arab, particularly Gulf, support for his cause. The struggle against Khomeini-ism, he argued, was neither a personal vendetta nor solely an Iraqi venture. Rather, it was a defense of the eastern flank of the Arab world against a violent and aggressive enemy. Should Iraq fail to contain the Iranians at the gates of the Arab world, it would not be the only casualty of the Iranian Revolution; the entire Gulf would be devoured by the fundamentalist Persians.

These claims fell on receptive ears. From his early days in power, Khomeini did not conceal his contempt for the Gulf dynasties and his determination to uproot them. "Islam proclaims monarchy and hereditary succession wrong and invalid," he declared, setting in train a huge wave of Shi'ite restiveness throughout the Gulf. In these distressing circumstances the Gulf monarchies found it increasingly difficult to decline the "protection" offered by their strong "sister" to the north, Iraq, who, only half a decade earlier, had openly demanded their heads. A brief and decisive military encounter, they apparently reasoned, would be the least of all evils. However risky, it might debilitate the two most formidable powers in the Gulf and curb Iran's messianic zeal.

Hence, in the summer of 1980 Kuwait openly sided with Baghdad, and during Saddam's first state visit to Saudi Arabia in August 1980 he apparently received King Khaled's blessing for the impending campaign against Iran. When war broke out, these two states quickly threw their support behind Iraq and their identification with the Iraqi cause grew as the Iranian threat loomed larger. By the end of 1981 Saudi Arabia had already extended some $10 billion worth of financial support to Iraq while Kuwait had contributed an additional $5 billion. During the war years this support reached some $50 billion, and it was evident that these loans were given with the knowledge that most, if not all, of them might not be repaid in the future. In addition, Saudi Arabia and Kuwait sold some oil on Iraq's behalf and allowed their ports to be used for the shipment of goods to and from Iraq, whose access to the Gulf had been severed at the beginning of the war. Saudi Arabia even allowed the use of its territory for the construction of an Iraqi oil pipeline to the Red Sea, thereby enabling Baghdad to bypass Iran's naval superiority and to export considerable amounts of oil. Although Saddam was never satisfied with the level of Saudi and Kuwaiti support and tended to accuse them (let alone the rest of the Gulf states) of being "free riders" on "Iraq's heroic struggle on behalf of the Arab nation," these contributions were undoubtedly critical to Iraq's war effort. Without Saudi and Kuwaiti financial aid and logistical support, Saddam's ability to weather Iraq's growing economic plight would have been seriously impaired.

Repressing Iraq's domestic opposition

In order to survive the window of extreme personal vulnerability to which he was exposed following Iraq's "voluntary withdrawal" from Iran in June 1982, Saddam exploited to the full his resourceful ruthlessness. In an attempt to inexorably implicate the Iraqi leadership in his policy, he took the unprecedented step of convening an extraordinary joint meeting of the Revolutionary Command Council (RCC), the Ba'th leadership and the military command in his absence, which pleaded with Iran for a ceasefire. The predictably dismissive Iranian response provided a fresh reminder, if such were needed, of the fate awaiting the entire Iraqi leadership in the event of an Iranian victory. Yet Saddam did not trust his associates, even under these extreme circumstances. During a special congress of Iraq's Ba'th Party, convened in late June 1982 after a lapse of eight years to reconfirm Hussein's absolute control over the party and state, he reshuffled the country's major power centers. Eight of the 16 members of the RCC were removed, as were a similar number of ministers. The army was more severely afflicted, with some 300 high-ranking officers executed during the summer of 1982, and many others purged.

Saddam also clamped down on the last remnants of Shi'ite opposition. In the spring of 1983 he arrested some 90 members of the prominent al-Hakim family, relatives of Hojjat al-Islam Mohammed Baqr al-Hakim, head of the Supreme Council of the Islamic Revolution of Iraq (SCIRI), an exiled military group trained and operated by Iran. Six of the detainees were executed, and the exiled leader received a personal message from Saddam threatening him with further executions should he continue his subversive activities; the threat was carried out two years later with the killing of ten other members of the al-Hakim family.

By that time, however, Shi'ite challenges to the regime had to all intents and purposes disappeared. In effect, the Shi'ites' behavior during the war demonstrated that Saddam's fears about the community's disloyalty had been grossly exaggerated. Not only did they fail to welcome their self-styled Iranian liberators, but they fought shoulder to shoulder with their Arab compatriots to rebuff the Iranian threat. Hence, with the exception of isolated terrorist activities that were easily contained, the Shi'ite community sealed its social contract with the Iraqi state with the blood of its sons. They just would not fight alongside the Iranians against their Arab brothers.

Had Saddam been aware of this Shi'ite state of mind in 1979 or 1980, the war might have been averted altogether. As things stood, he was able to accompany the sporadic repressive convulsions against the Shi'ite community with regular demonstrations of generosity. An important symbolic act of goodwill was the guarantee, both in the 1980 and 1984 elections to the Iraqi parliament, that some 40 percent of those elected would be Shi'ites and that the speaker of the 250-member legislature would also be a Shi'ite. On the material level, Saddam took much care to improve the standard of living of the Shi'ites and to renovate their holy shrines. Particular attention was paid to the tomb of Ali Ibn-Abi-Talib, the Shi'a's patron Imam, which was paved with special marble tiles imported from Italy.

Saddam also found the Kurdish threat during the early war years less ominous than previously believed. The tribal and linguistic fragmentation of the Kurdish community and the longstanding enmity between its two main resistance groups, Mas'ud Barzani's KDP and Jalal Talabani's PUK, precluded a joint Kurdish strategy and enabled the regime to pit them against one another. It was only after Iran had launched its first major offensive into Kurdistan in the summer of 1983 that the Kurdish opposition became a real irritant to the central regime. Yet even then Saddam managed to keep the two Kurdish organizations apart. While the KDP was brutally repressed, with some 8,000 members of the Barzani clan imprisoned, the PUK was carefully courted through substantial financial inducements and ambiguous political pledges. In late 1983 the talks between the government and the PUK culminated in a truce agreement. In the agreement, the contents of which have never been made officially public, the government reportedly agreed to hold "free and democratic elections" for legislative and executive councils of an autonomous region in Kurdistan, as well as to allocate 30 percent of the state budget to repair war damage. The PUK reciprocated by undertaking to form a 40,000-strong popular army "to protect Kurdistan against foreign enemies."

Before long, however, Talabani discovered that he had been double-crossed by Saddam, who had no intention whatsoever of rehabilitating Kurdistan or promoting Kurdish autonomy at the expense of the central government. Frustrated and angry, Talabani broke off dialogue with the authorities, buried his differences with Barzani and joined the KDP campaign against the regime. Thus, by early 1985, Saddam was confronted with a full-scale insurrection in Kurdistan. When his peace offer was spurned by the disillusioned Kurds, a ferocious campaign was launched against them. With the passage of time and the deterioration of Iraq's military position, this campaign assumed genocidal proportions. Not only were the 8,000 "prisoners" captured in 1983 executed, along with hundreds of other members of the Kurdish opposition, but the government embarked once more on a systematic effort to uproot the rebellious population from its native environment. By the end of the Iran–Iraq War in the summer of 1988, more than half of the villages and numerous towns in Kurdistan had been razed and their populations deported. Some half a million Kurds were placed either in easily controllable settlements in the vicinity of the main towns in Kurdistan, or in concentration camps in the south-western Iraqi desert.

The war and Iranian politics

Unlike the Iraqi regime, which did its utmost to shelter its people from the effects of war, the clerics in Tehran embraced the war with alacrity as an opportunity to rally the nation behind the revolution, eliminate domestic opposition, and promote Khomeini's vision of the worldwide export of Iran's Islamic message. Epitomized in the slogan "revolution before victory," this instrumental approach made the war from the outset an extension of the domestic political struggle, to which all military and operational considerations were subordinated. Thus, for example, Iran's abortive January 1981 offensive in Susangerd constituted a desperate bid by Bani Sadr, then President of the Islamic Republic and Commander-in-Chief of the armed forces, to shore up his fledgling position in relation to the mullahs. So intense was the enmity between them that the president considered the ruling Islamic Republican Party "a greater calamity for the country than the war with Iraq," while the latter maintained that "it is preferable to lose half of Iraq than for Bani Sadr to become the ruler."

Similarly, Iran's persistent adherence to human-wave tactics, despite their obvious futility and prohibitive cost, was motivated not so much by operational considerations as by the desire of the regime to strengthen the Pasdaran at the expense of the far more professional, albeit politically unreliable, military. Having entered the war without a reliable military institution of their own, the mullahs were grudgingly forced to rely on the military to contain the Iraqi invasion and to turn the tide of events. Yet they were not willing to grant it any trust or to give it much leeway in the conduct of operations, despite the devastating consequences of such distrust for Iranian national interests.

This of course was not how the war was presented to the Iranian public. To them it was described both as a trial of Iranian national resolve and commitment and as a holy crusade, so to speak, to protect Islam from the heretic Ba'th regime and its leader, Saddam Hussein. It was a relentless and uncompromising struggle against a vicious enemy, stretching to its limits Iran's

readiness for suffering, self-sacrifice and martyrdom. In Khomeini's words: "Victory is not achieved by swords, it can only be achieved by blood . . . it is achieved by strength of faith."

Khomeini knew all too well what he was talking about. While not unifying the nation overnight, the Iraqi invasion galvanized the unique combination of religious zeal and deep-rooted nationalist sentiment generated by the Islamic Revolution, and made Iranian

morale stronger and more stable than that of Iraq at both the operational and the national level. The willingness of the Iranian troops, particularly the Pasdaran and Basij, to incur high casualties and to undertake suicidal actions stood in obvious contrast to the Iraqi behavior and had a devastating effect on Iraqi morale, at least until mid-1982. Even after Iran realized that highly motivated and ill-equipped troops were not enough to achieve a military victory against

well-entrenched forces with massive fire support, it would still take years of sustained human-wave assaults for this revolutionary zeal to start fading away.

Yet the blind devotion of the Pasdaran and the Basij to the Islamic cause overshadowed the internal situation in Iran and portrayed Iranian society as much more cohesive and unified in its support of the war effort than it actually was. In fact, during most of the war Iran was considerably affected by internal divisions on different levels, which culminated at times in eruptions of violence that forced the government to divert part of its energies. The Kurds waged a continuous campaign against the central regime from early 1979, tying up regular forces in the north. Other domestic opposition groups, especially the left-wing *Mujaheddin e-Khalq*, challenged the authority of the revolutionary regime and resorted to sabotage and assassination. During 1981, for instance, the Mujaheddin assassinated some 1,200 religious and political leaders, many of whom were from the top echelons of the Islamic regime, while the government executed about 5,000 Mujaheddin guerrillas. In the later months of 1982, following the failure of successive Iranian incursions into Iraq, the confrontation between the Mujaheddin and the government brought Iran to the verge of civil war. Though far inferior in size and armament to the regime's various militias, notably the Pasdaran, the 20,000-strong Mujaheddin drew the country into an escalating vicious circle of violence, as car bombs and street battles in Iran's major cities claimed the lives of hundreds of innocent people. It was only in 1985, after a brutal campaign of repression, involving persecution, mass executions, imprisonment and the disappearance of activists and their family members, that the regime managed to get the Mujaheddin challenge under control.

The Iranian authorities took great pains to instill in their subjects the virtues of austerity and self-sacrifice. Here young Iranian girls make their contribution to the war effort. (Gamma)

Apart from this organized opposition, the high human cost of the abortive Iranian thrusts into Iraq, coupled with the deteriorating economic situation, generated widespread war-weariness and a decline in morale. This manifested itself in discontent, including a drop in the number of army volunteers after late 1984 and anti-war and anti-government demonstrations, most notably in mid-1985. Morale plunged sharply in 1987 as the regime responded inadequately to intensified Iraqi missile attacks on population centers. The decline in volunteers for the front assumed alarming proportions after the costly failure to capture Basra in the winter of 1987. Growing discontent among the poor, who constituted the mainstay of the regime's support, was particularly disconcerting for the clerics.

The regime tried to stem the mounting tide of public discontent by simultaneously appealing to national and religious sentiments and suppressing overt signs of opposition. Faced with the decline of morale, Khomeini issued a series of rulings as early as the autumn of 1982. In these he declared that parental permission was unnecessary for those going to the front, that volunteering for service was a religious obligation, and that serving in the forces took precedence over all other forms of work or study. At the same time, the regime mounted vigorous campaigns to encourage specific sectors (such as civil servants) to increase their war effort, inviting contributions, financial or in kind, from organizations and individuals. Many workers contributed one day's pay a month, and a list of donations to the war effort was published in the daily newspapers, with the value of gifts itemized against donors' names. The government also exploited the dispatch of Basij volunteers to the battlefront as a propaganda ploy, employing every conceivable means, from emotional and religious stimulation to financial inducements in order to increase the numbers of volunteers and financial contributions.

Those who would not contribute to the war effort of their free will, were forced to

do so. In October 1985 provisions were drawn up for sending government employees to the battlefront, up to 10 percent of them on full pay. Several months later, in the spring of 1986, plans were announced to give nearly 2 million civil servants on-the-job military training, and by the early summer emphasis had shifted to full mobilization of "all the forces and resources of the country for the war."

The war and the Iranian economy

An important role in this mobilization was played by economic factors. As the conflict was being transformed into a prolonged war of attrition, the chances of an Iranian victory had come to depend as much on the nation's relative tolerance of belt-tightening and self-denial as on its capacity for mass recruitment of zealous fighters. Unlike Iraq, which was at the height of an unprecedented boom when it initiated hostilities, Iran's economy was in the throes of rapid deterioration following the revolution. This deterioration was considerably accelerated during the war, as a sharp decline in oil revenues combined with the correspondingly steep rise in military expenditure to produce a large balance of payments deficit. Foreign exchange reserves, inherited from the previous regime, dropped from $14.6 billion in 1979 to a mere $1 billion at the end of 1981.

By way of overcoming these difficulties, the regime took great pains to increase Iran's oil production. Oil revenues rose strongly from $12 billion in 1981 to $19 billion in both 1982 and 1983, allowing the authorities to liberalize import restrictions so as to generate a revival in industrial and agricultural production. This success, however, proved short-lived. As Iraq intensified its economic warfare in 1984 with the initiation of the tanker war, Iran's economy took a sharp downward turn. Oil revenues dropped from $19 billion to $12–13 billion in 1984–85, then to

$6.6 billion in 1986. By 1987, nearly one in two Iranians had become unemployed.

The authorities fought this predicament with vigor and ingenuity. To service the agricultural sector at a time of total military mobilization, they established a mass organization titled The Reconstruction Campaign, whose members were exempted from military service and deployed in rural areas. They also cut non-essential imports to a minimum, thus saving precious foreign exchange, and sought alternative routes (notably through Turkey) for exporting Iranian oil. Foreign observers were greatly impressed by Iranian technicians, "masters of invention and innovation" in repairing damaged oil facilities, and by Iranian military plants "performing miracles" in making up for the severe shortages in Iran's military equipment.

There was, however, an instrumental, indeed cynical, side to the regime's handling of the economy. While doing its best to foster a sense of public acceptance of strict austerity measures, it was busy placating those constituencies deemed crucial to its survival by tailoring its economic policies to meet their needs. This applied not only to the regime's hard-core revolutionary followers and their families, who were generously remunerated for their service and suffering, but also to such bourgeois segments of Iranian society as the bazaar, whose economic resources were indispensable to the regime in its fight to keep austerity at bay. In 1984, for example, in a rare intervention in domestic policy

issues, Khomeini came out in favor of an economic policy that allowed the bazaar to retain control of trade, without excessive government interference.

This leniency stood in sharp contrast to the zeal with which the regime was suppressing all manifestations of organized dissent. Apart from the brutal repression of the Mujaheddin, the government clamped down on the Tudeh communist party, as well as on other political groups that posed, or seemed likely to pose, a threat to the authority and policies of the ruling Islamic Republican Party. The Kurdish rebellion had steadily ground down, and sporadic outbursts of street discontent (such as the 1985 incidents) were curbed with the aid of militant activists.

These repressive measures were, admittedly, a far cry from their Iraqi counterparts. While Saddam would not tolerate the slightest manifestation of dissent, the Iranian regime allowed a degree of institutionalized opposition, notably the Islamic Liberation Movement headed by the former Prime Minister Mehdi Bazargan. In early 1985, when the costly Iranian failures to breach the Iraqi lines combined with the war of the cities to stir public mutterings of discontent, Bazargan came out against the war, going so far (in a telegram to the United Nations Secretary-General) as to brand its continuation since mid-1982 as un-Islamic and illegal. And while this criticism had little effect on the Iranian public, it was nevertheless deemed by Khomeini as significant enough to deserve a personal rebuttal.

Death of a village

In the summer of 1988, fifteen-year-old Fakhir lived with his family in the small Iraqi Kurdish village of Koreme, some 31 miles (50 km) south of the Turkish border. Prior to the war, the village population had comprised some 150 families, but as the conflict came to engulf Kurdistan, most of the villagers moved out of Koreme to the relative safety of ravines a few miles away. Still, despite the ravages of war, including a number of attacks by the Iraqi army, Koreme remained very much intact as a village. Those inhabitants staying behind continued to cultivate their lands, while many of the escapees would come out at night to farm the fields nearest the ravines.

By this time, there were widespread reports of attacks on Kurdish villages and towns, on a different magnitude to anything that had taken place before. The Koreme villagers were not easily frightened, having endured destruction and death on numerous occasions. However, the horror stories they heard from fleeing Kurds were sufficiently alarming to convince them to undertake the difficult and risky flight on foot to Turkey—itself a highly uncertain haven for the Kurds. Their instincts were based on solid grounds. As the end of the war seemed in the offing, Saddam embarked on a massive punitive campaign in Kurdistan aimed at nothing less than the complete eradication of the Iraqi Kurds as a distinct socio-political community. Named the Anfal Campaign after a Koranic Sura, and commanded by Ali Hassan al-Majid, Saddam's paternal cousin, this operation reached heights of brutality that were exceptional even by the merciless standards of Saddam's Iraq. Like a steamroller crushing everything before it, the Iraqi army advanced throughout Kurdistan, indiscriminately spreading death and destruction. Villages were shelled or bombed,

at times with chemical weapons, before being stormed by the army. The villagers would then be rounded up. Women and children were separated from the men and sent to "hamlets" in Kurdistan that lacked basic humanitarian conditions. Men and boys were often summarily executed; others were dispatched to concentration camps in the south-western Iraqi desert, never to be seen again. By the time this horrendous campaign came to an end, in the autumn of 1988, thousands of villages and towns in Kurdistan had been demolished and their populations deported. Some half a million Kurds had been relocated, while another 250,000 had fled to Turkey and Iran.

In late August 1988, the Anfal Campaign reached Koreme in the form of aerial bombardments and constant shelling in the vicinity of the village. No chemical weapons were used in the village, but they were employed extensively at neighboring sites. On August 25–26, the main body of Koreme families, some 300 people, decided that the time had come for them to run for their lives. This, however, was easier said than done, as Iraqi artillery and helicopters were targeting the columns of fleeing Kurds to prevent them from reaching Turkey. And so, in the afternoon hours of August 28, the escapees were back in Koreme, only to be confronted with Iraqi forces.

A massacre in broad daylight

At the first sight of the soldiers, just outside the village, the men and boys lifted their hands to signal their surrender. To their great relief, they were not harmed but were instead separated into three groups—young and adult men, women and children, and old men—and taken into custody. The soldiers disarmed those with arms and searched them and the other men for any other weapons.

A smaller group of villagers was then separated from the group of young and adult men. A lieutenant told them to sit down, which they did. The other villagers, including those men not singled out, were led away behind the hill near the partly ruined village schoolhouse. As they were taken away, women and men screamed and cried out for their loved ones, and the soldiers tried to quiet them down. "We just want to ask them some questions," a soldier told the wife of one of the detained men. "Why do you think something is going to happen?" One of the officers approached the row of men, pulling aside those he apparently deemed too young. An argument developed over whether one boy was 12 or 13; he was eventually allowed to leave the group. One boy, who tried to stay with his father, was taken out of the line, as was a young teenager holding his baby sister in his arms. By the time this selection process had been finished, there were 33 men and teenage boys left in line.

Suspecting the bitter fate awaiting them, the men wept and pleaded for their lives, though the soldiers kept on insisting that nothing would happen to them. One of the officers even offered them cigarettes and water. Meanwhile, a dozen soldiers took up positions opposite the group. Some of them, too, were reassuring the men that they had no reason to worry. The commander, they said, was going to contact the local headquarters for instructions regarding their interrogation.

Shortly afterwards, one of the officers did precisely this. Speaking on his walkie-talkie, he reported capturing "armed subversives" and asked for instructions. The villagers could not hear the reply, but as soon as the officer put down the walkie-talkie, he turned around to the soldiers and ordered them to shoot.

The soldiers opened fire with their Kalashnikov AK-47 rifles on the 33 men squatting some few yards ahead of them. Some villagers were killed immediately, while others were wounded and a few were missed altogether. Having stopped shooting, several soldiers approached the line of slumped bodies on orders from an officer and fired additional individual rounds to ensure death. They then left the execution site without burying the bodies or touching them.

Surviving the firing squad

Surprisingly, despite the volume and close range of the firing, six of the 33 villagers managed to survive. One of them, a 34-year-old villager by the name of Aba, recalled being blown over backwards from his squatting position by the force of the bullet, which shattered bones in his leg, sending him rolling down a slope. He eventually fell into a stony ravine, where he remained lying on his back for 24 hours, partly visible and partly hidden by grass and stones. Occasionally during the night soldiers up the hill would take shots at him, but none bothered to come down, presumably because they thought he was dead.

Fakhir was even more fortunate than Aba. Finding himself in the execution line-up, together with two uncles (his father was not in the village at the time), he was taken out by a soldier, apparently because he looked younger than his age. This was indeed a major asset, as some of his friends perished at Koreme while others disappeared at a later stage. Even so, Fakhir came within a hairsbreadth of death during the forced relocation of the Koreme survivors following the executions. As the refugees reached the town of Salamia, Fakhir was asked by an officer for an identification card. His mother produced it, and upon seeing his date of birth—1973— the officer asked, "Why are you here? You are too old to be here." He then took Fakhir by the arm and walked him to the post at the main gate of Salamia security fort. At the main gate, Fakhir said, was an old man who had not been taken directly to the camps with the others. The old man said,

"Don't take this boy. Do him a good deed. Saddam didn't say you had to take this one." The officer hesitated, and the old man continued. "Saddam won't see if you don't take him. Saddam is not watching. Do good in the sight of Allah, the compassionate, the merciful." The officer let go of Fakhir, shook him roughly, and said, "Don't let me see you again. I was kind to you this once, but I won't be kind the next time."

Relocation of survivors

Although they did not see the execution, the rest of the villagers behind the hill heard the shots and knew exactly what they meant. Prevented by the soldiers from running back to their loved ones, women and men were weeping while the children screamed for their fathers. This made little impression on the soldiers, who herded the 150–300-strong group of mostly women, children and elderly out of the village. The bodies of the massacred lay where they had fallen, unburied, stiffened, and starting to swell in the summer heat. The soldiers then razed to the ground all of Koreme's residential homes, as well as its mosque and school. Power lines were pulled down and power poles knocked over. Orchards were burned, vineyards uprooted. The village springs were cemented over, and cement was poured into the wells.

Meanwhile the Koreme survivors were driven by foot to the district capital of Mengish, where they were locked up in the local fort, already bursting with thousands of Kurdish refugees from neighboring villages. Conditions at the site were appalling. Food was in short supply and many people went without water for several days, despite the scorching heat. Nor did the lot of the refugees improve after being moved several days later to the provincial fort of Dohuk. Some food and water was distributed, but it rarely amounted to more than a piece of bread every other day, handed out negligently. Water supplies were limited to a few barrels of hot water, placed in courtyards that were unsanitary, and insufficient to meet drinking needs. Some pregnant women miscarried and several boys died because of the dire conditions. A request by a pregnant woman to see a doctor was refused by a soldier on the grounds that "the Kurds have been brought here to die." Indeed, in a number of sweeps, the authorities removed all the remaining young and adult Koreme men from their families. They were then loaded on to army trucks that left Dohuk fort, never to be seen again.

The poisoned chalice

Iran's acceptance of the UN ceasefire resolution made little impression on Iraq. In his letter to the UN Secretary-General, Perez de Cuellar, President Khamenei demanded that Iraq be made to admit its responsibility for starting the war. While there was nothing new in this standard Iranian demand, which was apparently reiterated as a face-saving reason for the regime's dramatic U-turn, Saddam was not prepared to allow Iran to win the moral high ground. For years he had been pleading with the mullahs in Tehran for an end to hostilities, only to be contemptuously rebuffed time and again. Now that Iran had sunk to its lowest ebb in the war, Saddam was determined to make the best of it. Iraq rejected Iran's acceptance of the ceasefire as too ambiguous and demanded that it be explicitly and publicly endorsed by Khomeini in person.

By way of backing up this demand, on July 18 Iraq launched a series of air raids against strategic industrial plants in Ahvaz and Bandar e-Khomeini, and attacked Iran's nuclear reactor in Bushehr. Iran retaliated with strikes against Iraqi targets in Fao and the northern oil-rich area of Kirkuk, but it was evident that its weakened air force and missile stockpiles were no match for Iraq's formidable strategic capabilities. In recognition of this stark reality, Khomeini was grudgingly being pressured to suffer the ultimate humiliation and publicly announce his acceptance of a ceasefire.

The aged ayatollah, though, could not bring himself to break the bad news to his people. That was simply too much for the prophet of the "perpetual revolution" to bear. He was praying in his private mosque at his home while an announcer read the text of his message on the Islamic Republic's official radio station. It was 2 PM on July 20, and even though President Khameini had

announced Iran's acceptance of the ceasefire resolution three days earlier, Khomeini's message still came as a shock to the Iranian people. "Happy are those who have departed through martyrdom," ran the ayatollah's statement. "Unhappy am I that I still survive . . . Taking this decision is more deadly than drinking from a poisoned chalice. I submitted myself to Allah's will and took this drink for His satisfaction."

Yet Khomeini would not drink from the poisoned chalice without a bitter protest. "To me it would have been more bearable to accept death and martyrdom . . . [but I was forced to accept the advice of] all the high-ranking military experts." He pointed an accusatory finger in the direction of those forces deemed responsible for this shameful development, before concluding on a threatening note, "Accepting the [UN] resolution does not mean that the question of war has been solved. By declaring this decision, we have blunted the propaganda weapon of the world devourers against us. But one cannot forecast this course of events indefinitely."

This was, of course, not quite what Saddam had expected, and he raised the stakes still further. Although Resolution 598 called for a ceasefire as a first step towards a negotiated settlement, Iraq now demanded the immediate commencement of Iraqi–Iranian peace talks in advance. Tariq Aziz argued that Iraq considered that the war was still going on so long as Iran failed to clarify its intentions with regard to other aspects of the resolution, notably an exchange of prisoners-of-war. Iraq was eager to see the immediate return of its 70,000 war prisoners (compared to Iran's 45,000), as it would constitute proof of both the successful termination of hostilities and the beginning of Iraq's return to normality.

After Iran's acceptance of a ceasefire, Iraq allowed the
National Liberation Army, an Iranian dissident force
based in Iraqi territory, to mount an invasion of Iran.
(Gamma)

Since Aziz was effectively asking the
Iranians to set out their terms for a peace
settlement before a ceasefire had even been
agreed, the two belligerents remained locked
in three weeks of tough haggling,
punctuated by a string of military clashes.
Openly suspicious about Iran's motives, Iraq
continued to conduct limited offensive
operations in order to take more prisoners,
and, by occupying more Iranian territory,
improve its own negotiating position. This

during the war, this 90-mile (144 km) incursion was decisively defeated by the Pasdaran by the end of July, with the invading forces suffering heavy losses. Yet the Iranian regime was sufficiently alarmed to unleash a massive campaign of repression against the remnants of the Mujaheddin within Iran and their suspected sympathizers, involving thousands of arrests and executions.

Meanwhile, a large group of Iraq's international backers, from the United States and Western Europe to the Gulf states, were putting heavy pressure on Saddam to accept the ceasefire. At the same time, UN Secretary-General de Cuellar managed to convince the Iranians that the ceasefire should be immediately followed by face-to-face talks between the two countries. In an ironic reversal of roles, Iran, which for a year had stalled the implementation of Resolution 598, now became its vociferous proponent. Foreign Minister Velayati complained about Iraq's delaying tactics and urged the Security Council to take active measures against Baghdad. Hashemi-Rafsanjani argued that Iraq's continued aggression was proof, if any were needed, that Iran had been victimized by its neighbor.

These pressures brought the desired result, and on August 6 Saddam announced his readiness "for a ceasefire on the condition that Iran announces clearly, unequivocally and formally its acceptance to enter into direct negotiations with Iraq immediately after the ceasefire takes place." The following day, after some last-minute haggling, Iran accepted these terms.

On August 8, 1988, the UN Security Council convened and declared a ceasefire effective from dawn on August 20, and it was agreed that Iraqi and Iranian representatives would meet on August 24, under the auspices of the UN Secretary-General, to start their peace talks. A 350-strong force—the United Nations Iran-Iraq Military Observer Group (UNIMOG)—was established to monitor the implementation of the ceasefire, and the US Secretary of Defense, Frank Carlucci,

continued belligerence caused a brief resurgence of popular support in Iran for the war. So did the attempt by the Baghdad-based Mujaheddin e-Khalq's "National Liberation Army" to stage its own invasion of Iran, with armor and air and logistical support from the regular Iraqi military. The deepest penetration of Iranian territory

Tehran: Pasdaran Revolutionary Guards (SIPA Press)

announced that his country would shortly reduce its military presence in the Gulf.

Thus ended the Iran-Iraq War, one of the longest, bloodiest and costliest Third World armed conflicts in the 20th century. After eight years of bitter fighting, untold casualties, and immeasurable suffering and dislocation, the two combatants were forced, out of sheer exhaustion and debilitation, to settle for the *status quo ante* existing in September 1980. Yet there was little doubt that neither of them viewed the ceasefire as the end of the conflict. Consequently, both sides concentrated on rebuilding their armed forces against the eventuality of a new military conflagration, and accelerated the reconstruction of their economies and national infrastructures, a precondition for new military preparations. Both countries produced well over the 2 million barrels of oil per day assigned to them by OPEC. Iran re-opened its main terminal in Kharg Island to oil shippers and started rebuilding the devastated refinery at Abadan. Iraq embarked on a massive rehabilitation effort in Basra, resumed shipping from the port of Umm Qasr, and allowed a flow of consumer goods into the country.

The peace talks, although they began as scheduled on August 24, 1988, quickly ran into a blind alley, but continued inconclusively for the next two years. Eager to show his subjects the fruits of victory, Saddam insisted on Iraq's full control of the Shatt al-Arab waterway; he went so far as to threaten to dig a canal between the ports of Basra and Umm Qasr if this demand was not conceded. For its part, Iran insisted on Iraq's full compliance with the 1975 Algiers Agreement. As a result, all other aspects of the peace talks, notably the prisoners issue, remained deadlocked. Even a humanitarian attempt to exchange 1,500 sick and disabled prisoners in November 1988 failed to make any progress. The Iran–Iraq War may have ended, but a solution to Iranian–Iraqi enmity was not in sight.

A costly exercise in futility

The Iran–Iraq War is unlikely to be studied for its strategic lessons or battlefield accomplishments, but will rather be remembered as a costly exercise in futility resulting from the failure to apply most of the classic principles of war, from the adoption of realistic war aims to the conduct of the war itself. However, since military failure, no less than success, contributes to the development of military knowledge, the lessons of this war, with their very broad implications, particularly for the Middle East, cannot be overlooked.

Iraq's strategic miscalculation

One of the war's main ironies is that what was conceived as a limited campaign became the longest and bloodiest conflict between Third World states since the Second World War. The critical strategic error, and the one that caused the war's extension, was Iraq's failure to strike a balance between its foreign policy goals and its war strategy.

The most common explanation for this failure views the invasion of Iran as evidence of Saddam's unbridled regional ambitions, ranging from the occupation of Iranian territories (the Shatt al-Arab and Khuzestan), through the desire to inflict a decisive defeat on the Iranian Republic, to the need to assert Iraq as the pre-eminent Arab and Gulf state. By this line of argument, Iraq's inability to bring the war to a swift conclusion reflected the wide gap between these ambitious goals and the limitations of its military power. In other words, Iraq committed the common mistake of trying to bite off more than it could chew, having overestimated its own power and underestimated that of its opponent.

An alternative explanation maintains that failures in the implementation of national strategies do not necessarily stem from an underestimation of one's opponents but can equally arise from excessive timidity. Iraq did not misjudge the balance of power between itself and Iran prior to the war, for in the summer of 1980 it had an undeniable military edge. Nor did it appear to set its sights higher than its means permitted. Instead it assigned to its military forces tasks that were too limited. By failing to destroy a significant portion of the Iranian forces at a time when it was perfectly capable of doing so, Iraq laid itself open to counterattack and was thus unable to hold on to its limited territorial objectives. In other words, Iraq's grand strategy failed not because its military power was insufficient to the attainment of national goals but because too little was asked of it.

Be that as it may, the general conclusion, though obvious, is still worth restating. States should strive to keep the maximum degree of mutuality between their foreign-policy goals and the instruments employed to achieve them. They should opt to keep the widest possible security margins by preferring a strategy of general war in the pursuit of limited political goals rather than a strategy of a limited war for the attainment of far-reaching political goals. In his attempts to contain the Iranian threat to his personal rule, Saddam should have either avoided war altogether and tried to deflect the Iranian pressure by other means, or followed a strategy of general war in pursuit of limited aims. Such a strategy, had it been adopted, might still have failed, given the nature of the Iranian regime. But a strategy of limited war could only fail.

Operational lessons and implications

Broadly speaking, the Iran–Iraq War demonstrated that even non-conventional wars are won or lost by conventional means; that is, the level of competence in the application of the principles of war. Contrary to all appearances, Iran's operational successes in 1981–82 stemmed not from the blind devotion of the Pasdaran and the Basij but rather from the incorporation of these forces into comprehensive combined-arms operations, planned and carried out under professional military direction. When the conventional conduct of the war gave way to frontal human-wave assaults lacking any kind of inter-service co-operation, Iran failed time and again, and at an exorbitant cost, to breach the Iraqi defenses.

The war also underlined both the decisive impact and the severe limitations of air power in the modern battlefield. On the one hand, it afforded a convincing demonstration that chronic inferiority in this area is a strategic liability for which it is almost impossible to compensate in regular conventional warfare. On the other hand, the war showed that air power can hardly win wars on its own without the accompaniment of a decisive land campaign. On numerous occasions during the war Iraq used its vast air superiority to break the stalemate on the battlefield by extending the fighting to Iran's rear and driving the revolutionary regime into instinctive and ill-conceived reactions in a desperate bid to reduce the pressure from its population. Yet it was only when it managed to regroup its ground forces into a string of large offensives in 1988 that Iraq managed to bring the war to conclusion.

Finally, the Iran–Iraq War undermined several crucial thresholds and "red lines" in inter-state wars. It was the first armed conflict since the First World War to witness the extensive use of poison gas; it involved the most intensive campaign against non-belligerent shipping since the Second World War, and, also, perhaps, the harshest attacks on population centers and economic targets. These escalations entailed far-reaching adverse implications for Middle Eastern stability. With the breaking of so many taboos, and the exceptionally cavalier international response to Iraq's massive use of poison gas, every regional army facing the possibility of war must now be aware that the international accords barring the use of chemical weapons and other non-conventional weapons are apparently of little binding value, as are the international norms pertaining to military attacks on civilian targets. Indeed, the Iran–Iraq War has significantly accelerated the already alarming regional arms race, with Syria and Libya (not to speak of Iran and Iraq) developing substantial chemical weapons capabilities in addition to their continued interest in procuring more surface-to-surface missiles. Even Saudi Arabia has purchased long-range ballistic missiles from China.

The tempering of Iran's revolutionary zeal

The inconclusive termination of the war, with no clear victor, constituted a triumph for the *status quo* powers over a formidable force of revisionism. Not only did Iran fail to topple the Ba'th regime and thus set in train a wave of religious radicalism throughout the Middle East, but its vision of an Islamic order was widely spurned by most Sunni fundamentalists. Only in Lebanon does Iran's version of Islamic fundamentalism appear to have left a lasting impact, with the rise of militant Shi'ite movements such as Amal and Hizbullah, but even there it has been constrained by domestic and external factors, such as Syrian domination of the country. It would be no exaggeration to argue that with the confinement of the revolution to Iran's boundaries the Middle Eastern state-system has withstood one of the gravest ideological challenges to its existence.

True, the *status quo* powers can hardly relax: religious radicalism is subdued but not eradicated. Rooted in the region's millenarian Islamic tradition, and reinforced by the wider Third World trend to seek refuge in religion from the alienating forces of modernization, Islamic fundamentalism did not originate in the Iranian Revolution and neither do its fortunes depend exclusively on domestic developments within Iran. Yet, considering that Iran has been the foremost standard bearer of political Islam since the demise of the Ottoman Empire, its actions and inaction are likely to play an important role in the vicissitudes of this phenomenon. And in this respect there is little doubt that the Iran–Iraq War exerted a profoundly sobering and moderating influence.

To the Islamic Republic of Iran, like the First French Republic and the newly established Bolshevik state, war was the main means to gaining national legitimacy and rallying popular support behind the regime. The war was also a struggle for absolute stakes. If the Iraqis had ever entertained thoughts of undermining the revolutionary regime in Iran, by 1988 they had long since relinquished them. In contrast, the Islamic Republic displayed an unshaken commitment to the concept of "war until victory" (which implied the overthrow of the Ba'th regime) up to the very last days of the fighting.

Iran's acceptance of Security Council Resolution 598 was therefore no tactical matter but rather a decision of the highest strategic order: the war was brought to an end in order to preserve the very revolution that had given birth to it. By the time Iran announced its readiness to end the war and enter into peace negotiations with Iraq, its regional worldview had come full circle: from the revisionist dream of shaping the Gulf (and the wider Middle East) along

Islamic lines, to acquiescence in the regional *status quo* established by the Shah in 1975; from the vision of "the permanent revolution" to the notion of "Islam in one country." True, Khomeini's vision of an Islamic *umma* did not disappear from the Iranian vocabulary, but the far-reaching goal of subverting the regional order had succumbed to eight years of futile conflict, giving way to the conventional "rules of the game" to which the Islamic Republic had been so adamantly opposed.

Emerging from the war as a crippled nation, Iran faced the Sisyphean task of reconstructing its devastated social, economic and military systems. The ceasefire was followed by a heated debate among the clerics over whether to allow greater room for the private sector in the reconstruction effort and to accept foreign aid to this end. By and large the pragmatists, who advocated a more open Iranian economy, had the upper hand over the more doctrinaire faction, though their position was to suffer occasional setbacks with the vicissitudes of Iran's domestic and external position.

Iran also embarked on a vigorous, and highly successful campaign to end its international isolation and return to the mainstream of international politics, effectively discarding the ideological precept of "neither East nor West" that had guided the revolution from its very inception, in favor of a pragmatic policy of courting both East and West. Relations with the Soviet Union, which had plunged to their lowest ebb in 1983 following the suppression of the Tudeh Party, began to warm in 1986 with the revival of the bilateral Permanent Commission for Joint Economic Cooperation. This improvement gained considerable momentum from mid-1987 onwards as Iran saw in the USSR a major counterbalance to the growing US naval presence in the Gulf.

The end of hostilities also enabled Iran to mend fences with the Western powers following the severe setback of 1987: diplomatic relations with France were restored in June 1988, with Canada a month later, and with Britain in December. Relations with West Germany, already warmer than with the rest of the Western European powers, grew closer with a visit by Foreign Minister Hans-Dietrich Genscher to Iran in November 1988. The renewed honeymoon with the West was temporarily curtailed in February 1989, following a religious ruling by Khomeini, calling for the execution of the British author Salman Rushdie for writing allegedly blasphemous passages in his novel *The Satanic Verses*. Yet even at that moment of mounting passions Iran did not abandon caution, and displayed a measure of restraint. Thus, for example, Khomeini's call for Rushdie's execution was paralleled by milder voices indicating possible ways to avert crisis.

Regional reactions

With the threat of Islamic fundamentalism apparently receding, the Arab monarchies of the Gulf, Iraq's staunch supporters throughout the war, began to distance themselves from overt animosity towards Iran. In late September 1988, Kuwait re-established diplomatic relations with Tehran, and a fortnight later Bahrain and Iran agreed to upgrade diplomatic relations. Even Saudi Arabia, which severed diplomatic relations with Iran in April 1988, reacted favorably to Iranian overtures: on October 25, 1988, in response to a conciliatory statement by Speaker of the parliament Hashemi-Rafsanjani, King Fahd ordered the state-controlled media to halt their propaganda attacks on Iran.

Yet not all Middle Eastern states welcomed the ending of the war. Turkey, for one, had very few reasons to rejoice over the ceasefire, given its substantial gains from the war. In the economic sphere, a significant increase in Turkish trade with both belligerents had immeasurably improved the outlook of the country's crisis-ridden economy. Strategically, Turkey's importance in the region, already boosted

after the Iranian Revolution and the consequent loss of Western strategic assets there, was further enhanced by the war in general, indeed by the very thought of an Iranian victory. For Turkey, therefore, the post-war era involved diminishing gains and new challenges.

But the major loser from the ending of the war was undoubtedly Iraq's neighbor to the west, Syria. Animosity between the Syrian and Iraqi ruling Ba'th parties pre-dated the outbreak of the war and manifested itself in mutual subversive and terrorist activities, as well as harsh propaganda campaigns; on several occasions in the mid- and late 1970s the two countries came close to war. During the Iran–Iraq War Syria became Iran's staunchest ally, curtailing Iraq's war effort to some extent, something that Saddam neither forgot nor forgave. Once hostilities were over he sought to settle the account with Damascus through interference in its own backyard: Lebanon. The closing months of 1988 witnessed the development of substantial Iraqi support, in the form of money and arms, to the Christian Maronites, who only a few years earlier had been Israel's closest allies. Iraq was even reported to have used the Israeli port of Haifa for arms deliveries to the Maronites, with Saddam stating his readiness to co-operate with Israel for the "liberation of Lebanon."

No less anathema to the Syrians was the apparent moderation of Arab attitudes towards Israel produced by the war. Tehran's relentless commitment to the substitution of its militant brand of Islamic order for the existing *status quo*, its reluctance to end the war before the overthrow of the Ba'th regime in Baghdad, and its subversive and terrorist campaign against the Gulf monarchies had convinced many Arabs that the Iranian threat exceeded by far the Israeli danger and that there was no adequate substitute for Egypt at the helm of the Arab world. Hence, before 1980 was out, Saddam, who a year earlier had triumphantly hosted the Baghdad Summit, which expelled Egypt from the Arab League for its peace with

Syria's President Hafiz al-Asad, an erstwhile enemy of
Saddam Hussein, became Iran's foremost Arab supporter
during the war. (Gamma)

Israel, was pleading with the excommunicated
Egyptian president Anwar Sadat for military
support. As Egypt developed into an
important military and economic provider,
Saddam would tirelessly toil to pave the
way for its re-incorporation into the Arab
fold, regardless of its peace treaty with
Israel. By the end of the 1980s, Egypt had
already regained its pivotal role in the Arab
world, with its moderate policy becoming
the mainstream Arab line and its former
detractors seeking its friendship and
protection. In May 1989, Egypt took part in
the all-Arab summit in Casablanca for the
first time since its expulsion from the Arab
League a decade earlier.

The road to Kuwait

Alongside its moderating consequences,
the Iran–Iraq War exerted a profoundly
destabilizing impact on regional, and
indeed world, affairs in that it sowed the
seeds of Iraq's occupation of Kuwait and the
ensuing 1991 Gulf War.

Though the Iraqi regime went out of its
way to portray the end of the war as a
shining victory, the truth was that Iraq, no
less than Iran, emerged from the eight-year
conflict a crippled nation. At least 200,000
Iraqis had lost their lives, while about
400,000 had been wounded and some
70,000 taken prisoner: an exorbitant price
for a nation of 17 million people. In 1980
Iraq could boast a $35 billion foreign
exchange reserve; eight years later it had
accumulated a foreign debt of some $80
billion—roughly twice the size of its Gross
National Product. This debt was extremely
disturbing, since repayment arrears and the
consequent reluctance of foreign companies
and governments to extend further credits
meant that the reconstruction of Iraq from
the destruction wrought by the war would
have to be shelved.

Economic estimates put the cost of
reconstruction at $230 billion. Even if one
adopted the most optimistic (and highly
unrealistic) assumption that every dollar of
oil revenues would be directed to the
reconstruction effort, it would have taken
nearly two decades to repair the total
damage. As things were a year after the
termination of hostilities, Iraq's oil revenues
of $13 billion did not suffice even to cover
ongoing expenditure: with civilian imports
approximating to $12 billion ($3 billion
for foodstuffs), military imports exceeding
$5 billion, debt repayments totaling some
$5 billion, and transfers by foreign workers
topping $1 billion, the regime needed an
extra $10 billion per annum to balance its
current deficit, before it could even think of
reconstruction; and this without
taking into account the substantial
domestic economic costs, such as the
$2.5–$7.9-billion defense expenditure.

Nor could Saddam make even the
slightest progress on the most important
foreign policy issue: a peace agreement with
Iran. The UN-orchestrated peace talks in
Geneva quickly ran into a dead end;
successive Iraqi initiatives using both the
carrot and the stick led nowhere. With the
lack of progress Saddam was forced to look
to his guns. The formidable army remained
by and large mobilized, costing the destitute
Iraqi treasury a fortune. With the war over,
conscripts began questioning the necessity
for their continued mobilization. Saddam's
attempt to defuse this seething social
problem by ordering partial demobilization
in 1989 backfired, as it proved beyond the
capacity of the shaky Iraqi economy to
absorb the huge numbers of young men
pouring into the labor market.

By 1990, Saddam had realized that even
though the war might have ended, the
struggle for his political survival had entered
a new, and equally dangerous phase. The
nature of the threat to his regime had, of
course, fundamentally changed. Tehran was
no longer demanding his downfall, at least
not for the foreseeable future. Instead, he
faced the potential risk of the Iraqi people

Iraqi forces invade Kuwait on August 2, 1990, making it
the latest casualty of the Iran–Iraq War. (Rex Features)

rising against him, should he fail to deliver
the promised fruits of the "historic victory."
An immediate economic breakthrough had
thus become, literally, a matter of life and
death, and who was better poised to
provide this breakthrough than tiny and
wealthy Kuwait?

At a summit meeting in Amman in
February 1990, Saddam asked King Hussein
of Jordan and President Mubarak of Egypt
to inform the Gulf states that Iraq was not
only adamant on a complete moratorium
on its wartime loans but urgently needed an

immediate infusion of additional funds of
some $30 billion. "Let the Gulf regimes
know," he added, "that if they will not give
this money to me, I will know how to get
it." The message was immediately passed to
Saudi Arabia by the Jordanian monarch.

The same month, during a working visit
to Kuwait, the Iraqi Oil Minister pressured
his hosts to abide by the new oil quota set
by OPEC earlier that year. He then proceeded
to Riyadh to deliver a personal message from
Saddam to King Fahd: the Saudis must
convince the rest of the Gulf states not to
exceed their oil quotas. This had little
influence on Kuwait and the United Arab
Emirates (UAE). Instead of reducing their oil

quota to make more room for increased Iraqi production they continued to exceed their quotas by far, putting a downward pressure on world oil prices.

By July 1990, Saddam's frustration with Kuwait was intense. He was now determined to extract substantial grants plus a complete moratorium on war loans on top of adherence to OPEC quotas. The Kuwaiti indifference to his desperate needs amounted to "stabbing Iraq in the back with a poisoned dagger." He felt that he had gone out of his way to plead the Iraqi case and further begging would only cause him (and, by extension, Iraq) an unendurable public humiliation.

He began to put his strategy in place. On July 15 a division of the elite Republican Guard began moving from central Iraq to the south-east of the country, just north of Kuwait. Within 24 hours some 10,000 men and 300 tanks were in place and a second division was making its appearance. By July 19, 35,000 men from three divisions had been deployed near the Kuwaiti border, and the military build-up was continuing apace.

As the military build-up got under way the diplomatic offensive began. On July 16 the Iraqi Foreign Minister, Tariq Aziz, delivered a memorandum to the Secretary-General of the Arab League for distribution to the League's members. In this he accused Kuwait both of deliberately causing a glut in the oil market (allegedly costing Iraq some $89 billion between 1981 and 1990), and of directly robbing Iraq by "setting up oil installations in the southern section of the Iraqi al-Rumaila oil-field and extracting oil from it." By way of redressing these wrongs and helping Iraq recover from the dire economic plight that it now faced because of its defense of the Arab nation from the Iranian aggression, Aziz demanded the raising of oil prices to over $25 a barrel; the cessation of Kuwaiti "theft" of Iraqi oil; a complete moratorium on Iraq's wartime loans; and the formation of "an Arab plan similar to the Marshall Plan to compensate Iraq for some of the losses during the war."

The next day Saddam escalated further by publicly accusing Kuwait of conspiring with "world imperialism and Zionism" to "cut off the livelihood of the Arab nation," and threatening that Iraq would not be able to put up with such behavior for much longer. "If words fail to afford us protection," he warned, "then we will have no choice but to resort to effective action to put things right and ensure the restitution of our rights."

The Kuwaiti Cabinet met the day after Saddam's speech. The prevailing view was that surrender to such extortionist demands would only lead to unlimited demands in the future that would make Kuwaiti sovereignty merely nominal. They suspected that some concessions might be necessary, but were determined to reduce them to the barest minimum. If they were going to do a deal with Iraq they wanted in return abandonment of Iraq's claim over Kuwait. However startled it may have been by the harsh Iraqi rhetoric, the Kuwaiti leadership remained complacent, interpreting the Iraqi demands as a bargaining position rather than an ultimatum. Thus, within less than 24 hours from Saddam's speech, Kuwait had already dispatched to the Secretary-General of the Arab League a strongly-worded memorandum refuting the Iraqi accusations and expressing strong indignation at Iraq's behavior.

The defiant Kuwaiti response to his threat confirmed Saddam's perception of the emirate as a parasitic state thriving on Iraq's heavy sacrifices, that would never meet its fraternal responsibilities without physical coercion. At a meeting on July 25, 1990, with the US Ambassador to Baghdad, April Glaspie, he warned that Iraq could not hold back indefinitely.

We are not going to do anything until we meet [with the Kuwaitis]. If, when we meet, we see that there is hope, nothing will happen. But if we are unable to find a solution, then it will be natural that Iraq will not accept death, even though wisdom is above everything else.

Having misinterpreted Glaspie's mild response to his threats as a "green light" to settle the scores with Kuwait, Saddam accelerated the deployment of Iraqi forces along the border, and on August 2 invaded Kuwait. The Iran–Iraq War had claimed its latest casualty.

Glossary

abrogate To formally cancel or abolish through an act of authority.

appease To pacify or make peace with (often by sacrificing principles).

armament A military force; a collection of weapons.

belligerent Inclined to combativeness; a person or country engaged in battle.

circumspect Careful to consider all circumstances.

consolidate To join together into a whole.

contingency An event that may but is not certain to occur.

coup A decisive takeover.

disseminate To spread around.

incursion Hostile entrance into a territory.

infantry Soldiers trained, armed, and equipped to fight on foot.

logistics The handling of the details of an operation.

onerous Laborious or burdensome, especially because of being distasteful.

pre-empt To seize upon to the exclusion of others.

proximate Near or next to in space, time, or order.

purge To get rid of.

regime A government in power.

For More Information

The American Institute of Iranian Studies
Dr. Erica Ehrenberg
Executive Director
118 Riverside Drive
New York, NY 10024
Web site: http://www.simorgh-aiis.org/
smain.htm
The American Institute of Iranian Studies is a nonprofit, nongovernmental overseas research organization that seeks to support the advancement of knowledge and understanding of Iran and Iranian culture and civilization.

Council on Foreign Relations
New York Office
The Harold Pratt House
58 East 68th Street
New York, NY 10065
(212) 434-9400
Web site: http://www.cfr.org
Founded in 1921, CFR is a nonpartisan organization dedicated to studying foreign relations and making resources available to those of similar interests. Its Web site provides information on various regions, including the Middle East.

Middle East Outreach Council
Jean Campbell
Associate Director, Middle East Studies Center
Portland State University
P.O Box 751
Portland, OR 97207-0751
(503) 725-8566
Web site: http://socialscience.tjc.edu/mkho/
MEOC/index.htm
With a target audience of nonspecialists at the K-12 and college levels, the MEOC is a national nonprofit organization "working to increase public knowledge about the peoples places, and cultures of the Middle East, including the Arab world, Israel, Iran, Turkey, and Afghanistan."

**Middle East Studies Association
of North America, Inc.**
1219 N. Santa Rita Avenue
The University of Arizona
Tucson, AZ 85721
(520) 621-5850
Web site: http://mesa.wns.ccit.arizona.edu
According to its Web site, the Middle East Studies Association (MESA) is "a non-political association that fosters the study of the Middle East, promotes high standards of scholarship and teaching, and encourages public understanding of the region and its peoples through programs, publications and services that enhance education, further intellectual exchange, recognize professional distinction, and defend academic freedom."

Science and Arts Foundation
1010 Rockville Pike, Suite 506
Rockville, MD 20852
(301) 340-2525
Web site: http://www.science-arts.org
The Science and Arts Foundation has brought the Internet to over one hundred model state schools, universities, orphanages, and cultural institutions in deprived areas of Iran. The Web site also provides links to online educational projects.

United Nations Headquarters
First Avenue at 46th Street
New York, NY 10017
Web site: http://www.un.org
The United Nations is an international organization made up of 192 member

states. It refers to itself as the "town hall of global affairs." The headquarters in New York provides exhibits and other resources. The Web site provides information about all areas of the world.

Web Sites

Due to the changing nature of Internet links, Rosen Publishing has developed an online list of Web sites related to the subject of this book. This site is updated regularly. Please use this link to access the list:

http://www.rosenlinks.com/eshi/irir

For Further Reading

Abdulghani, Jasim. *Iraq and Iran: The Years of Crisis*. Baltimore, MD: Johns Hopkins University Press, 1984.

Brown, Ian. *Khomeini's Forgotten Sons: The Story of Iran's Boy Soldiers*. London, England: Grey Seal Books, 1990.

Bullock, John, and Harvey Morris. *The Gulf War: Its Origins, History, and Consequences*. London, England: Methuen, 1990.

Cordesman, Anthony. *The Iran-Iraq War and Western Society*. London, England: Jane's Publishing Co., 1987.

Grummon, S. R. *The Iran-Iraq War: Islam Embattled*. New York, NY: Praeger, 1982.

Karsh, Efraim. *The Iran-Iraq War: A Military Analysis*. London, England: International Institute for Strategic Studies, 1987.

King, Ralph. *The Iran-Iraq War: The Political Implications*. London, England: International Institute for Strategic Studies, 1988.

Pelletierre, Stephen. *The Iran-Iraq War: Chaos in a Vacuum*. New York, NY: Praeger, 1992.

Index

About the Author

Efraim Karsh is a professor and head of the
Mediterranean Studies Program at King's
College, University of London. He has held
various academic posts at the Sorbonne, the
London School of Economics, Columbia
University, Helsinki University, and Tel-Aviv
University. Professor Karsh has published
extensively on Middle Eastern affairs, Soviet
foreign policy, and European neutrality.